Not What I Expected

"A superb book. Chock-full of arresting insights as well as warmth and wisdom." —Edward Hallowell, MD, author of *The Childhood Roots of Adult Happiness*

"Full of relatable stories and accessible grounding science, *Not What I Expected* offers parents validation, empathy, and practical tools. A deeply personal read. Readers may feel as if they're sitting with Dr. Eichenstein, who is all at once understanding them, challenging them, and leading them to acceptance and empowerment in their roles as parents."

—Dr. Tina Payne Bryson, coauthor of the *New York Times* bestselling books *The Whole-Brain Child* and *No-Drama Discipline*

"At last, a book that speaks directly to parents of children who are atypical, as well as to their teachers. Easily digestible and offering insight, support, warmth, and a touch of humor, *Not What I Expected* will enhance your parenting toolbox and enrich your parenting life."

—Betsy Brown Braun, MA, child development and behavior specialist, and bestselling author of *Just Tell Me What to Say* and *You're Not the Boss of Me*

"A gem of a book. Dr. Rita Eichenstein has written with remarkable insight and compassion about the rarely focused on problems of the parents and family members of learning disabled or atypical children. A must-read for practitioners as well as parents."

—Marion Solomon, PhD, author of *Lean on Me* and *The Wonder of We in a Culture of Me*

"Clear, practical, and filled with hope, the ideas and practices in this book offer a science-based common-sense approach that any parent or practitioner working with an atypical child will be benefit from. What better gift can we give these children!"

—Elisha Goldstein, PhD, author of *Uncovering Happiness* and *The Now Effect*

"With an enormous amount of experience, and mastery of the atypical brain, Dr. Eichenstein provides a road map for understanding and thriving alongside your atypical child. *Not What I Expected* is a must-have for any parent who has an atypical child and/or any professional who works with special needs families."

—Dr. Charles Sophy, psychiatrist and medical director for the County of Los Angeles Department of Children and Family Services

W9-BUM-456

continued . . .

Not What I Expected

Help and Hope for Parents
of Atypical Children

. . .

Rita Eichenstein, PhD

A PERIGEE BOOK

A PERIGEE BOOK
Published by the Penguin Group
Penguin Group (USA) LLC
375 Hudson Street, New York, New York 10014

USA • Canada • UK • Ireland • Australia • New Zealand • India • South Africa • China

penguin.com

A Penguin Random House Company

NOT WHAT I EXPECTED

ISBN: 978-0-399-17176-5

An application to catalog this book has been submitted to the Library of Congress.

First edition: April 2015

PRINTED IN THE UNITED STATES OF AMERICA

10   9   8   7   6   5   4   3   2

Every effort has been made to ensure that the information contained in this book is complete and
accurate. However, neither the publisher nor the author is engaged in rendering professional advice
or services to the individual reader. The ideas, procedures, and suggestions contained in this book are
not intended as a substitute for consulting with your physician. All matters regarding your health
require medical supervision. Neither the author nor the publisher shall be liable or responsible
for any loss or damage allegedly arising from any information or suggestion in this book.

While the author has made every effort to provide accurate telephone numbers, Internet addresses,
and other contact information at the time of publication, neither the publisher nor the author assumes any
responsibility for errors, or for changes that occur after publication. Further, the publisher does not have any
control over and does not assume any responsibility for author or third-party websites or their content.

Most Perigee books are available at special quantity discounts for bulk purchases for sales
promotions, premiums, fund-raising, or educational use. Special books, or book excerpts, can also
be created to fit specific needs. For details, write: Special.Markets@us.penguingroup.com.

To Izzy, who is the inspiration of all good things

To David and Erin, Josh, and Deanie,
who have been my greatest teachers and spiritual guides

And to Carly June, who will lead us all

CONTENTS

CHAPTER THREE

Anger and Blame 73

CHAPTER FOUR

Bargaining and Seeking Solutions: "I Promise to Be the Best Mommy in the World" 127

CHAPTER FIVE

The Depression Trap 157

CHAPTER SIX

Active Acceptance: Joyful and Purposeful Living 197

FOREWORD

The journey from infancy to adulthood is both promising and perilous—a path best navigated with the informed and loving support of parents and other caregivers along the way. As such an important figure in your child's growth, how can you best be informed and prepared to optimize the support and guidance you give? And when things don't go as planned, when a child has an unanticipated difference in how they think, feel, or behave—when they are "not typical"—how can you be as strong and knowledgeable as possible in order to offer the best support you can? When things get tough, how can you remain a wellspring of love for your child? Our own resistance, confusion, and disappointment, and sometimes our embarrassment and shame when we compare our family to the experiences of others, can create stress and may distance any of us, at least at first, from being present for our child in the most supportive ways we can.

The term "atypical child" is now commonly used to describe individuals who have some features that make their particular patterns of growth; ways of thinking, perceiving, and feeling; and ways of behaving and interacting with others not what we usually expect. Whether this atypical way of being stems from a difference in the body or in the brain's structure and functioning, the difference is not the result of anything a parent has intentionally done. Yet often we can feel guilty and responsible for these differences. Parental care and concern are deep, innate feelings that can sometimes become overwhelming, restricting our thinking and making our mood somber and our optimism dimmed. Learning to understand your own emotions can help free you from these common yet unnecessary internal reactions.

In this magnificent handbook for learning to become the best source of support for an atypical child, Rita Eichenstein, PhD, serves as an inspiring guide. This book will walk you step by step through the inner and outer challenges of this journey. As a clinical neuropsychologist with extensive experience and knowledge, Dr. Eichenstein supports you not only with her expertise with atypically developing children and adolescents, but also with her emotionally supportive strategies. If you've just found out about the unique challenges for your child's development, this is a powerful guide to help you take on this new information. And if you've been living for a while with knowledge of your child's atypical development, this book will also be of great help in guiding you through the long-term issues you will face.

Not What I Expected itself is wonderfully not what you may typically expect from a book on this topic: Instead of focusing exclusively on your child's experience and needs, the approach explores the scientifically established view that the best way to support your child's development is to encourage and support your inner understanding. By paying attention to your own feelings and reactions, you can catalyze the transition from first sensing that something is different and seeking professional help to adjusting to this new knowledge and then learning to move from the common experiences of denial, anger, sadness, and grief toward a sense of acceptance, mental clarity, and empowerment.

Take in the wisdom and support *Not What I Expected* provides so that you and your child can optimize your relationship and flourish, both together and as individuals living your best possible lives.

—Daniel J. Siegel, MD
Executive director of the Mindsight Institute
Clinical professor at the UCLA School of Medicine
Author of *Brainstorm* and *The Developing Mind*
and coauthor of *Parenting from the Inside Out*,
The Whole-Brain Child, and *No Drama Discipline*

INTRODUCTION

Welcome to a book about parenting that does not focus on your child. Instead, it focuses on the most important force behind your child's well-being: you, the parent. I wrote this book to help you learn how to cope with your feelings about parenting a child who is different from what you expected—what I term as an atypical child.

What does atypical mean? It's a term that encompasses children who do not conform to the usual expectations, whether because of a learning disorder, behavioral or psychological issues, medical problem, or another condition. Atypical also refers to kids who do not meet criteria for a specific diagnostic category, or who have not yet been diagnosed. They might be quirky, delayed, difficult, or just unusual. They might be highly gifted in one area but delayed in others. Their suffering, and the suffering of their parents, does not get a label. All of these children's struggles generate intense feelings in their parents—feelings like bewilderment, confusion, anxiety, and fear.

I meet these parents when they come to me to get their children tested. As a neuropsychologist, I'm trained to conduct assessments of a child's brain-behavior connections. Every day, worried parents ask me, "What am I doing wrong? What am I supposed to do? Please help me understand my child better."

What they don't ask, but what I've discovered that many are thinking, is: *Am I a bad person? What's wrong with me? I don't know how to handle my feelings about my child. I feel crazy because no one believes me when I say something's wrong with my kid.* Or more commonly, *My child is driving me crazy and I feel like a terrible parent, but it's my feelings that are the hardest part, not my child.* Some parents have fears they don't dare verbalize: *Am I causing this? Was it something I ate during pregnancy?* And many have anxieties they try to suppress, but which bubble up every night in the wee hours: *What am I supposed to do with my feelings? Am I entitled to my feelings? Isn't it supposed to be about my child, who is clearly suffering?*

This book is designed to help parents of atypical children understand what they are feeling and learn how to manage their emotions. The difficult feelings involved in parenting special children are normal responses that evolve in predictable phases. Many of parents' most painful or shameful feelings are innate, brain-based reactions to stressful or traumatic situations. There are techniques you can use to manage the emotional phases you will pass through when coming to terms with raising your atypical child. By learning how to handle these difficult but common emotional and cognitive states, you'll be able to maximize your ability to parent your child wholeheartedly. When parents understand and have control over a seemingly uncontrollable situation, they become empowered and their confidence grows.

Raising an atypical child requires atypical parenting. It involves an ongoing process of self-questioning and decision making that can overwhelm even the most committed parents. The responsibility for this young life is in your hands, yet you may often feel helpless and ill-equipped to track down all the options and juggle the demands of doctors, teachers, therapists, and social workers, not to mention family members. In addition to these obvious stressors, there are deeper issues. Having an atypical child will trigger emotions that are hardwired in all of us—denial, fear, bargaining with fate, isolation, and depression—along with hope, optimism, and joy.

As a neuropsychologist who has worked with thousands of families, I believe that the secret crisis of atypical children is the crisis of their parents. Parents, both as individuals and as couples, often struggle to keep their lives together while helping their children. Mothers in particular are at a higher risk of depression than the average mom. Divorce is rampant among couples with special-needs or difficult children. Everyone knows that raising atypical kids takes a heavy toll on parents, but until recently few have recognized how much the parents' mental health impacts their children's well-

> **Raising an atypical child requires atypical parenting.**

being. Historically, dealing with parents has not been a focus of pediatric medicine. Parents' emotions are usually ignored, sometimes even when a life-altering diagnosis is delivered. As one parent noted, "The doctors gave me a diagnosis and a brochure and sent me on my way. It took me a long time to handle the impact of the information, let alone to be able to be helpful to my child."[1]

A growing body of research now confirms that parents' moods can affect the way they care for their children and how those children fare.[2] Yet health providers have not acted on the news.

Children's advocate and author Dr. Perri Klass wrote, "As a pediatrician, I tend to focus on the child, of course. Asking mental health questions of the parent can sometimes feel intrusive or invasive."[3] The child's welfare is naturally a front and center concern, but who ensures that this child is nurtured and protected? Who needs to be consistently upbeat and encouraging? It's usually the parent. And what about that parent? How is he or she coping with this child and these challenges?

How are you? How are you holding up? Where is the road map to help you navigate your own journey?

Parents Are Not Robots

I decided to write *Not What I Expected* after many years of working with both children and parents in psychotherapy, doing neuropsychological assessments and helping parents understand their children. These latter sessions would often run over two hours as we pored over the test results, discussed my impressions, and determined how the overall profile would impact their child and what they could do to help. After these long meetings, I would advise the parents to go home, relax, read over the report again, and take some time to digest the information. I would promise to call in a few days or weeks to see how the family was doing.

But many parents did not go home and proceed as planned. Instead, they fell into a state of paralysis and denial and delayed acting on the information. When I called to check in, they often seemed dazed, upset, or confused. How can they be confused, I used to wonder, when we spent so much time reviewing everything?

I came to realize a very important truth that all clinicians need to understand: Parents are not robots who can automatically deliver a menu of services to their child. They are human, with needs of their own. And when it comes to discussing their child's diagnosis, something in their brain shuts down, making them unable to process the distressing information. As I continued to work with parents over many years, I saw that the different emotional states they passed through deeply impacted how they related to their children, the treatment decisions they made, and how their children fared.

I wanted to learn how to help these parents manage their feelings, so I looked high and low for information on the topic—and found nothing. I was astonished that a subject so critical to the well-being of special children was simply absent. No books, no websites, no magazines devoted exclusively to the complicated and profound emotional challenges that all parents of atypical kids face. So I set about writing such a book myself.

Why Understanding Your Emotions
Makes You a Better Parent

Good parents take care of their own needs as well as those of their children. They have worked through their emotional minefields and therefore have a better array of responses for their family. The fact is, your emotional well-being is crucial to your child's future. Understanding your emotions gives you a measure of control over yourself and the daunting situations you encounter. It helps you relate positively to your child and your family. Your emotions also impact your decision making, and for parents of atypical kids, important decisions crop up regularly. Your mental state sets the tone for healthy (or unhealthy) parenting and affects your child's ability to form loving attachments. As a parent, you have a serious responsibility to maintain your own emotional inner balance. The emotional impact that you will have on your child is directly related to how well you understand and process your own feelings and reactions. Only then can you mindfully tune your parenting antenna outward in a controlled and reflective manner.

Children, even infants, are exquisitely sensitive to their parents' moods and reactions. Your words can't disguise your true feelings—if you tell your child, "I'm so happy to see you today, honey!" but don't mean it, your child will know. And most children will assume that they are the cause of your stress or unhappiness. While it's true that atypical children create more stressful conditions for parents, that doesn't mean your emotions must be permanently pushed out of whack. We all have the capacity to intentionally improve our emotional balance, but first we must understand our feelings, know where they are coming from, and learn what to do with them.

> We all have the capacity to intentionally improve our emotional balance.

This book is intended not only for parents of kids with developmental, psychological, or learning disorders but also for any parent who has children that seem to challenge the typical parenting parameters. Whatever your child's condition, in order to survive the labyrinth of parenting challenges and decisions that lie ahead, you will need to understand what you are going through emotionally and acquire the tools to deal with those emotions.

Emotional Phases You Can Expect

When a child is diagnosed with any type of condition, or even before a diagnosis, parents' emotions surge into overdrive. While all parents are continually battling fear and anxiety about the well-being of their child, parents of atypical children will go through a series of neurologically based ("hardwired") emotional reactions before their psychological responses and connection to their child becomes stabilized. There are at least five feeling states that parents often experience:

1. Denial/retreat
2. Anger/aggression
3. Bargaining/seeking control/seeking solutions
4. Depression/isolation/shame
5. Acceptance/equanimity/integration

Some parents experience all of these feeling states; others go directly to one feeling state and get stuck there. The emotional phases are sometimes sequential; in other families the parents shift in and out of different phases at different times. The process is not logical, and the phases can feel turbulent and chaotic even though the range of responses is predictable. This emotional journey, and how you can eventually pass through it to reach a place of mindful equanimity and stability, is what I will explain and illustrate in this book. I use a brain-based model to demonstrate what goes on in the minds and psyches of parents as they process information about their child.

In the opening chapter, you'll learn how parents' expectation of raising a perfect child is shattered when their son or daughter is diagnosed or their development or personality disrupts general expectations. We'll look at how a parent's mental health and self-esteem is affected when a child is found to be atypical. In subsequent chapters, you'll learn about the five major phases you can expect to pass though as you come to terms with your real child. As I guide you through the ways you may feel and behave during a particular phase, I'll share related cases from my client files (they are all composites—my clients' confidentiality is sacred). I'll also offer techniques for focusing, coping, and calming yourself, so that you will be able to move forward with compassion and energy.

Throughout this book you will read vignettes about children with a variety of diagnoses. Some of these are found in the DSM-5 (*Diagnostic and Statistical Manual of Mental Disorders, Fifth Edition*), others are in the ICD-9 (*International Classification of Diseases, Ninth Revision*), and other diagnoses, such as sensory processing disorder and auditory processing disorder, and nonverbal learning disorder (NVLD) do not fall within the realm of psychology, psychiatry, or neuropsychology. They are treated by other health professionals, such as occupational therapists, audiologists, and speech and language therapists. The professional world acknowledges that these conditions or clusters of symptoms that seem to look like a disorder exist, but there is disagreement about what to call them. And in some cases, there is no exact treatment protocol that is universally recognized as the "right" treatment. And in some cases, children are just quirky or nondiagnosed.

The insights and suggestions in this book are based on my own clinical experience as well as the work of experts in the fields of emotional development, parenting, neuropsychology, and neurobiology, including Daniel J. Siegel, Jaak Panksepp, Pat Ogden, Martin

Seligman, Elisha Goldstein, Jon Kabat-Zinn, Bessel A. van der Kolk, Kristin Neff, Richard Davidson, and Linda Graham, among many others. Their research reveals how much we all have in common: our imperfections and frailties, our ability to adapt, our fears, our resilience, our bravery. While your atypical child may have come as a huge surprise to you, I will bet that in the end, the biggest revelation will be how well you rise to the occasion. Maybe sputtering and flailing around a bit—but you will rise! And you'll carry your child with you. As you go through this essential process of learning about yourself, I hope you will consider me your companion, cheerleader, and confidante.

—Rita Eichenstein, PhD
Los Angeles, 2015

CHAPTER ONE

What We Expect When We're Expecting

Letting Go of the Ideal Child

Even before I got pregnant I had an image of what my child would be like. She—it was always a she!—would be calm and sensitive, like me. Outgoing but also studious and creative—which are also traits that I have. I'm ashamed to admit all of this now. But when we found out that our son (!) has a learning disability, the diagnosis, combined with his wild, rambunctious behavior, threw me into a deep depression. It was like I had lost something that I never really had to begin with.

—Emily, parent of an 8-year-old with ADHD and dyslexia*

• • •

Most of us conjure a distinct image of our future child when we contemplate parenthood. We not only want our child to be smart, good-looking, confident, happy, talented, and charming, we

*All of the people whose stories appear in this book are composites. They are not representations of specific men, women, or children. The confidentiality of my work is extremely important to me and to my clients. In the case of people who agreed to have their names mentioned, I have included a first and last name.

expect those things, and much more, because parents-to-be can't help but imagine the best of all possible outcomes. If we are artistically inclined, we might imagine finger painting with our child or taking her to the museum. If we are athletic, we envision playing catch on the lawn or shooting hoops at the park. Even if we had no specific daydreams about our baby before he or she arrived, the fantasy may have materialized during the infant or toddler years—the vision of a precocious child picking out an original tune on the piano or setting up a wildly successful lemonade stand. Such imaginary parent-child scenarios are perfectly natural, because it's part of our genetically programmed DNA to pass down aspects of ourselves and our culture to the next generation. We are predisposed to want to share our interests and strengths with our children.

In addition, there is plenty of societal pressure to produce not an average child, but an exceptional one. Keeping up with the Joneses' baby requires more than just comparing how fast our child is growing and how soon she learns to sit up, crawl, walk, and talk. Today's moms and dads often feel compelled to try to teach their baby to read before she's three (never mind how unlikely and unnecessary that is). Other parents buy apps for baby sign language, toddler puzzles and quizzes, preschool reading and writing games, and more. With all this focus on early achievement, how can expectant parents *not* conjure an ideal child? Anything less would be a child who is sadly unable to compete in today's precarious economy.

Cultural expectations greatly contribute to how we form the image of our ideal child, but so do personal expectations: a beautiful little girl who will grow up to attend Northwestern and become a doctor like her mom . . . a sociable little boy who has the makings of a successful business leader like his uncle Joe. Spoken or not, acknowledged or subconscious, we all have dreams of the future child, teen, and adult that our baby will grow up to be.

While the rational part of our brain insists that we will be happy with any child as long as he or she is healthy, the emotional part—our heart and our imagination—tells us something else. It's no wonder, then, that a small riot lets loose in a corner of our brain when these expectations are disrupted because our child is in some way atypical. A voice protests: *What's happening? This is* not *what I expected!*

Learning That Your Child Is Different

Experience has taught me that it is impossible to predict parents' reactions to the news that their child is atypical. Initially, their outward response may be plucky: "Okay, what can we do?" Or they may retreat into denial: "This can't be true!" But whatever they say out loud, I know that their internal reaction is much deeper and less rational. Parents commonly struggle with fear, anger, denial, sadness, shame, and resentment. Underlying each of these emotions is a profound sense of loss that, unfortunately, is rarely acknowledged by pediatricians, mental health professionals, or well-meaning family and friends. What exactly has been lost? The fantasy of the perfect child, the child who was supposed to evolve from that perfect cherub a parent falls in love with in the first few days of life. The child they imagine will reflect the very best of Mom and Dad.

Some children I see in my practice are delayed, hyperactive, or struggling to master the demands of their external world. Some are physically ill. Some are depressed, anxious, are on the autism spectrum, or are highly sensitive, tightly wound, or quirky. Some are quite gifted in certain ways but are delayed in other areas. And some kids are just different. Or difficult. Their parents typically ask for an assessment in order to understand their children better and to figure out how to help them. They are often at a point of exasperation, if not despair. Yet I find all of the children (with rare exceptions) to be endearing and extremely interesting. And so many I find to be quite unique and promising in their own way.

I spend a lot of time with the children in my practice, getting to know them, figuring out how they learn, what makes them happy, how they cope with their challenges. Spending so much time with these kids, I become very attached to every one of them. I can see beyond their atypicality to *who they are*. To me, it is always awe-inspiring because I know that this world needs all types of minds. The most amazing and game-changing contributions have come from atypical and unique individuals who did not fit into the narrow expectations of current societal and academic norms. I look for the gifts behind the disability and the potential in each child. These kids, I sometimes marvel, are going to be our future leaders. Movers and shakers. Innovators and healers. I truly believe that each child has a gift to offer.

You might think the toughest part of my job is telling parents what is "wrong" with their child. And sometimes it is. But often the harder part is convincing parents that, although there might be a delay or a diagnosis, their son or daughter nevertheless has many wonderful attributes and genuine strengths. I see the faces of discouraged, frightened, or angry parents, faces that tell me so much about what I'm up against. Many parents don't believe me. Some are hostile. Many are on the brink of tears. Their reasoning brain has temporarily shut down and they are flooded with emotional reactivity. These parents, and thousands like them, are experiencing something that has only recently been acknowledged and named: They are grieving. They're grieving the loss of their idealized child. These mothers and fathers are grappling with the inexplicable feeling that, as Emily put it, "Something has been lost that I never really had to begin with." A parent's sense of loss and the accompanying emotional reactions can be devastating.

> "Something has been lost that I never really had to begin with."

If you are the parent of a child who is atypical, you know what I'm talking about. And I know what you're going through. I want to help you navigate your way through the emotional minefields that families like yours encounter, so that you can become more comfortable with your life and more supportive of your child. Parents need to understand their own reactions. They need to know that they are not alone, and that what they feel follows a universal and predictable sequence. I hope that as you come to understand the emotions that arise as you parent your atypical child, you will not only become stronger and more relaxed, you will become a better parent.

Are You Ashamed to Admit You're Disappointed?

We not only expect to have ideal children, we expect ourselves to be ideal parents, and ideal parents are not supposed to be disappointed when they discover that their child is different. If you are like most parents, you may believe you're supposed to take your child's differences or diagnoses in stride and be grateful for your uniquely wonderful son or daughter, regardless of the behavioral, learning, or medical challenges that disrupt your life every day. You may think you are not allowed to feel angry, resentful, or sad even if your child's condition affects the quality of his life, where she is going to school, who he can play with, the quality of the family's life, and your own plans for the future. You may try to suppress your disappointment and condemn yourself because you believe it means you are selfish, uncaring, and unkind.

Admitting that you can't give up the image of your ideal child—that every day you catch yourself falling into a quagmire of "what-ifs"—may leave you feeling terribly guilty. You may wonder why you are not the parent you want to be, and you may beat yourself up over it. Disappointed in yourself as a parent, it's likely that you nonetheless cannot shake the other disappointment, the one that is reflected in the enduring mental picture of the little boy or girl who does not have the problems your son or daughter has. That imagined child was supposed to materialize, but now he or she never will. And you probably feel ashamed of yourself for even thinking such thoughts.

News flash: It's normal to feel this way!

In the 1950s, the psychologist Carl Rogers developed the idea that there are three basic aspects of self-concept. I believe these are transferred to how we view our children, and that they can help us make sense of our conflicted and guilty feelings about parenting an atypical child. They are:

1. Self-image: the view we have of ourselves.
2. Self-esteem: how much value we place on ourselves.
3. Ideal self: what we wish we were really like.

As parents, we inadvertently see our kids as an extension of our own self-image. Our self-esteem tends to rise and fall according to things such as which preschool our child gets accepted to, how fast he learns to read, how many awards she wins, and so on. And our ideal self is threatened when we recognize that our child is not ideal. With our sense of self all wound up in our child, it's no wonder that we become profoundly conflicted when that child does not meet our expectations—no matter how lofty and unrealistic they may have been in the first place.

In their book *Parenting from the Inside Out*, Daniel J. Siegel and Mary Hartzell note that we bring our own emotional baggage to our role of parenting, and this can influence our relationship with our children in unpredictable ways. Many parents had issues similar to the ones their children have, and the idea that their child will have to suffer from these issues like they did can leave parents feeling heartbroken and worried. Your relationship with your child can be affected by these and other unresolved issues in your own life, and this may also affect the way you react to a child who does not live up to your expectations.[1]

We human beings are hardwired to want to feel safe and connected to the community around us. When we have a child who is different, it can make us feel as if our position among our friends and the larger society is suddenly threatened. At the same time, we may love our child fiercely and be extremely fearful for him or her. Having an atypical child evokes different emotions in different parents. While some avoid, deny, or search for someone to blame, others hover and overprotect to the point of hindering the child's natural development.

Your conscious or unconscious fantasy of having an ideal child is a normal part of being a parent. It's normal to have great expectations for your son or daughter, and to feel sad when those expectations are threatened. It is part of your own internal need to find perfection in your world. And that's fine—it's human; it's just not realistic. There is a term in humanistic psychology called *congruence*, which means accepting that our real self and our ideal self are very different, a gap that can be a source of psychological suffering. We will talk about acceptance later in this book. For now, and possibly for the first time since you suspected that your child had a difference, give yourself permission to feel the sadness and disappointment that you may have been suppressing. Let it be okay to feel that way in this moment. Then, when you're ready, take a deep breath and be open to the opportunities for hope and joy that this child, along with his or her differences, will bring to your world.

Letting Your Feelings Out

Why is it so important to acknowledge your disappointment as well as all your other feelings? Because when you suppress or deny those feelings, the denial turns into anger that is directed either inward or outward. Anger directed outward can turn into aggression. Aggressive anger may take the form of criticizing, ridiculing, or otherwise lashing out at your spouse, your child, or others. Anger that is directed inward can turn into depression and increased sensitivity to stressors. Some parents who turn inward shut down emotionally.

I have seen a number of parents who do not want to deal with their feelings regularly belittling their child. Or screaming at each other. Or blaming the school and switching schools abruptly. Or shutting professionals out and not being able to get the help for their child that he or she needs. No well-meaning parent wants to be the cause of their child's distress, and yet parents' unacknowledged, unresolved emotions can cause them to do just that.

On the other hand, when parents are in touch with how they're feeling and can work through their emotions, their self-awareness and self-care creates a safe haven for their child. And that is the ultimate goal. Acknowledging and dealing with your feelings—even the so-called negative ones—is important not only so you feel better about yourself but also so you can better guide and nurture your child.

Sometimes one negative feeling can cover up another that is even more difficult to face. Lyle, the father of a young boy diagnosed with autism, admitted to feeling disconnected from and cold toward his son. "I just can't relate to him, so I kind of shut off when I'm around him," he told me. I explained to Lyle that if he felt cold and detached toward his child, it was important to figure out why. Underneath "cold and detached" is usually anxiety or anger. So Lyle had to consider why he might be angry. Did it make him angry that he had the added burden of parenting a special-needs child? Was he angry at his family and friends for failing to understand his son's condition? Was he anxious that he in some way caused this? Was he too worried about his son to connect emotionally—was it easier to "shut off" than to confront his feelings?

Parents of atypical children often fear that their own emotions are not only shameful, they are also abnormal. Mara, whose five-year-old daughter had significant learning differences, confided to me that she felt "really guilty for feeling this way," but that she was jealous and resentful of her neighbor whose kids did not have the challenges Mara's daughter had. "Here she is complaining about being overwhelmed just because she has to chauffeur her daughters to piano lessons and soccer practice—and meanwhile I'm stuck taking my little girl from one doctor to the next, to all types of remedial therapies. I don't want to resent my neighbor and feel bitter, but I do. Is it normal to feel this way?"

After I reassured Mara that her feelings were definitely not uncommon, she asked me what other emotions were experienced by parents like her. I told her, "Look at the feelings chart hanging on the wall. Every single negative feeling on that chart can crop up for parents of atypical kids."

I keep a feelings chart in my office for many reasons, but one of the most important is to remind parents that what they're going through emotionally is not unusual. I want them to know that they do not have to fear that those negative emotions are shameful or embarrassing. And I want you to know that as well. To the contrary, being open about what you're feeling, at least to yourself in private, is the start of a healthy process that will benefit you, your child, and the entire extended family. Of course you will not want to share negative feelings with your child, and you'll want to be careful that the adults you confide in will be discreet. But honestly admitting your feelings to yourself is an important step you need to take.

Inside the Brain of a Parent

Logic may tell us that no one is perfect, but nothing about parenting is logical. Our response to learning that our child is atypical is rarely logical either. Yet pediatricians, teachers, and school administrators often deal with parents in a rational, logical, practical way: *This is your child's problem. This is the solution.* Or even harder: *We don't know what to do with your kid, but he sure has a problem—please go home and fix it!*

If only it were that easy! It took me years to realize that many parents of atypical children, upon hearing a diagnosis or a teacher's suggestion that their child be tested, are too overwhelmed by their emotions to be able to quickly take the appropriate steps. That's because the "emotional brain" naturally takes over in traumatic situations. There is a biological explanation for this response.

Parenting skills arise from a fine interplay between several areas of the brain. Emotional surges from the limbic system (the emotional part of our brain) are balanced against the more sophisticated neocortex (the thinking part of our brain) to make rational decisions and respond flexibly, with both empathy and insight. Primitive caregiving instincts to nurture and protect our young originate in the limbic system, while the neocortex gives us skills that are unique to humans: reflection, regulation of our emotions, and intuition (the ability to read emotions in others), or what Daniel Siegel calls *mindsight*.[2] The limbic system is referred to as the emotional brain, the neocortex as the thinking brain. When parents have heightened anxiety, the limbic system (the emotional brain) suppresses the functions of the neocortex (the thinking brain).

The emotional brain is not only responsive to negative input. It also gives us remarkable experiences: It facilitates our parent-child attachments, our appreciation and creation of music, art, and poetry, our imagination, our sense of wonder, and our joy at the sight of a sunset or our newborn child. However, if our brain becomes overloaded by stressful or traumatic experiences, it starts to misfire and we lose the ability to strike a balance between emotional surges and logical problem solving. Depending on our level of resilience and how deeply we react to unexpected traumas, reactions to finding out about a problem with our child can impact our nervous system and in turn our body functions: Our heart rate can speed up, we can begin to hyperventilate, and our digestive region can become uncomfortable. Losing our emotional balance can be an immediate and short-lived reaction or it can persist for an extended period.

Part of the reason for this is that stress floods the brain with the chemical cortisol, which activates the limbic system and suppresses the middle prefrontal cortex, the area responsible for calming, regulating, and balancing emotions and thinking. Brain chemicals are powerful agents that affect our response to our children, for good and for ill. Hormones such as oxytocin, vasopressin, and prolactin are "parenting drugs" that enable mothers and fathers to fall in love with their child and maintain strong ongoing nurturing patterns. But when the brain senses a threat—for instance, our child's impending meltdown in the parking lot, a looming diagnosis, or a call from the principal's office—our cortisol levels surge and our mind goes into a primitive fight-or-flight response. Our ability to parent reasonably (via a balancing act between our limbic system and our neocortex) and lovingly (due to hormonal surges) becomes suppressed. Our functioning may become chaotic as we are bombarded by feelings, fears, anxieties, and defenses. Some people shut down and become catatonic in face of the external chaos, losing their ability to function in normal activities. Luckily, most adults are not in that state for too long, having learned techniques to quiet their minds and control their emotions. Adult society is predicated on the assumption that we are in control of our emotional brains and can make reasonable and prosocial choices.

But that is not always the case.

For example, if I found out that my neighbor's child had autism, the problem-solving part of my brain would light up and I would immediately think about referring the parents to an excellent social skills center in the neighborhood. However, if that diagnosis were suddenly about *my* child, solutions might not pop up so easily. My anguished emotions would flood my reasoning brain and all systems would temporarily shut down until I could find my internal equilibrium. I might even become relatively dysfunctional, crying or yelling a lot. My limbic system would hijack the logical, reasoning part of my brain. I would be experiencing a personal trauma.

When your child seems different or isn't learning normally, your expectations are disrupted. And whenever your expectations are disrupted, there is some level of trauma. In a sense, everything about raising an atypical child is so loaded with stress that any deviation from the expected script is bound to trigger a traumatic response from the parents. Some parents are more resilient than others, and people do react differently to similar experiences. But trauma will always disrupt the reasonable response, thus changing parental behavior.

Five Emotional Phases to Expect

It may surprise you to know that the word to describe what most parents experience when given their child's diagnosis is *grief.* Using words like *grief* or *loss* may seem overly dramatic, but while the loss of your ideal child doesn't compare to the experience of actually losing a loved one, it is a loss nonetheless. As a parent of an atypical child, you are in a unique category. You have "lost" the idealized child you had expected to parent, and to some extent you believe you will be losing the typical family life that you anticipated. Underneath the grief, you may be feeling scared and vulnerable.

Recent scientific studies suggest that repressing or denying your emotions is unlikely to make them go away, but becoming aware of what you are feeling in the moment and being able to talk about it helps tremendously when it comes to managing your emotions. Research has found that when you name your negative emotions, there is a shift in their intensity.[3] Your anxiety lessens and you feel calmer. This important neuroscience discovery comes with a catchy slogan, "Name it to tame it." If you can mindfully put words to your emotional state without judging it, you allow yourself to grow to the next level, hopefully to a place that is more resilient and better able to cope with the challenges.

In my work with parents of atypical children, I have seen that they go through a series of emotional phases as they deal with the disruption of their expectations and acclimate to the reality of their child's condition. These phases in some ways parallel Elisabeth Kübler-Ross's five stages of grief, but there are important differences, the most obvious being that no actual death has occurred. These phases are more fluid, with parents often moving in and out of the various feeling states several times over the course of a month, a week, or sometimes even a day. Parents may experience some but not all of the phases. The five phases are:

1. Denial/retreat
2. Anger/aggression
3. Bargaining/seeking control/seeking solutions
4. Depression/isolation/shame
5. Active acceptance/equanimity/integration

The five phases can be experienced out of order, simultaneously, or repeatedly over months or years, until you come to acceptance. In addition, two parents may experience the phases at different times, perhaps in a different order, or one of the two parents may not experience a particular phase at all. Complicating things further, Mom, Dad, grandparents, stepparents, and close relatives all form one unit, and within that unit there will be some people who are denying, some who are bargaining, some who are angry, some who are accepting. And each of those people can vacillate. If you are not aware of this phenomenon, you may find it hard to stay focused and keep moving forward with your child's care.

What's important is that you recognize the phases in yourself and in others. Let's say you're coming home from the doctor and you just learned that your son has difficulty processing auditory language. You try to explain this to Grandpa and he responds, "No way! That's ridiculous. He hears me just fine." Grandpa might be caught in denial. If you recognize that it is a phase, you can avoid wasting energy being angry with him. Instead of getting frustrated, discouraged, or angry at Grandpa, you can acknowledge his opinion, show him some websites or reading material about the condition, and have a conversation with him.

The same thing is true of your own feelings—your first mission is to recognize them. What to do after that is the topic of the rest of this book. Let's now take a look at each of the five phases.

Phase 1: Denial/Retreat

Often a parent's first response upon learning that a child may have a developmental condition is to flatly deny it. This is a normal reaction to try to minimize overwhelming emotions. Denial is a defense mechanism that protects us from emotions we may not be able to handle. Therefore, when we hear a diagnosis we find terribly upsetting, we may block out the words or disregard the person who delivers them.

Denial is usually a temporary response that gives way to acknowledging that there is, in fact, a problem. Initially, however, a parent in denial who learns that his son has attention deficit/hyperactivity disorder (ADHD), for example, might respond by saying something such as "There is nothing wrong with our son! Boys will be boys, and he's just acting like a normal six-year-old." I call this response the "deer-in-the-headlights" phase, and in the next chapter, I'll explain what happens in your brain during this period.

There are many permutations of denial. Sometimes one parent accepts, the other denies. Sometimes Mom suspects something is wrong but denies that it is as serious as it really is. Or the parents deny the extent of therapy needed: "Yes, he has dyslexia, but we're not going to need a special tutor. I can work with him myself." And sometimes the parents are well aware of the problem, but close relatives will argue with them.

> ### DEFINITION: DYSLEXIA
>
> Dyslexia is a learning disability characterized by problems in the acquisition of reading, spelling, writing, speaking, or listening. The National Institutes of Health estimates that about 15 percent of the United States population is affected by learning disabilities, mostly with problems in language and reading. The condition appears in all ages, races, and income levels. Dyslexia is not a disease, but describes rather a different kind of mind that learns in a different way from other people. Many people with the condition are gifted and very productive; dyslexia is not at all linked to low intelligence. In fact, dyslexia has nothing to do with intelligence. Studies show that individuals with dyslexia process information in a different area of the brain than do non-dyslexics. Treatment of dyslexia requires a systematic intensive intervention plan.

Phase 2: Anger/Aggression

As the masking effects of denial begin to wear off, the parent is confronted with the reality of the situation. Since it can be painful to face the fact that your child has a serious problem, the pain is typically redirected and expressed as anger. Friends, family, teachers, complete strangers—even inanimate objects—can become the target of a parent's anger, as can the child him- or herself. It is vitally important to recognize when you are in the anger phase because your anger can impair key relationships and even lead to divorce. An angry parent who has not managed to get past this phase is often perceived as "difficult" by doctors and teachers. I call this the "roaring momma-bear phase" and will explain why it is so hard to be rational at this time.

Phase 3: Bargaining/Seeking Control/Seeking Solutions

A common response to feelings of helplessness and vulnerability is an urgent need to gain control over the problem. Parents of atypical children may express this need by coming up with ways to "bargain" or negotiate with the diagnosis in order to mitigate its effects and consequences. For example, parents might try to gain control over their child's developmental disability by searching for a special diet or an alternative breakthrough treatment featured in the news or on the Internet. While it is commendable to want to do all you can to help your child, you must also learn how to spot phony research claims and make informed decisions before selecting a treatment. Acknowledging that you may be in the bargaining phase can help you become more cautious as you seek appropriate treatment for your child. I term this the "human phase" and will explain why, from a brain-based perspective, it is the most cognitive (that is, the least emotionally reactive), yet it is not without pitfalls.

Phase 4: Depression/Isolation/Shame

When the reality of a child's diagnosis sinks in, parents are understandably overwhelmed and may become depressed over myriad issues. Common among the questions plaguing parents:

- Is my child's problem something I caused or could have prevented—or something my child inherited from me?
- Will I be up to the stresses and challenges of raising an atypical child?
- Will we be able to afford the best treatment for our child?
- Am I ignoring our other child/children by focusing on our atypical child?
- Will the relationship with my spouse suffer because we have different ideas about how to deal with our child's problem?

Often contributing to a parent's depression is a profound sense of isolation. You may be the only one of your friends with an atypical child and thus have no one with whom to share your worries and concerns. In my clinical practice, I frequently hear parents say:

"No one understands what I'm going through."

"I feel so alone, so isolated."

"How can I tell the neighbors that our child won't be going to the public school with their kids?"

"I don't feel comfortable discussing our child's problem with my own parents."

And then there is the lingering sadness over the loss of the ideal child, causing further depression. Parents may continue to compare what their family life could have been with what they believe it will now be. Accompanying that sadness is shame that they are still stuck in the past, as well as shame that their family is not like all the others. Some families come from cultures where shame (and guilt) are associated with being negatively evaluated (either by oneself or others). Because of an atypical child, the family may have failed to meet imagined societal standards. For example, research has found that in Chinese families, individuals are more likely to feel ashamed and guilty in response to a family member's "transgression."[4]

Understanding what happens in the brain of a vulnerable and hurting parent is essential if you are to recognize it in yourself and move into a more healing frame of mind.

Phase 5: Active Acceptance/Equanimity/Integration

Not everyone reaches this phase. It takes work, as many of my clients can attest. The dignity and grace shown by a number of parents with whom I have worked is truly inspiring. Coping with the reality that your child is different is a deeply personal experience. Although nobody can fully understand all the emotions you're going through, getting the support you need—including the coping strategies found in this book—will help you attain an inner equanimity and an acceptance of the unique and very real child whose parent you are. In the chapter on active acceptance, I will share with you success stories of atypical children and their families, so you can gain some perspective on the situation. A diagnosis or a condition marks the start of a process, not an end point in the game of life.

Betty and Bob: Surf's Upended

Realizing that you are going to experience at least some of these emotional phases gives you a road map for the territory you are about to enter. That's not to say it will necessarily be an easy trip, but I can guarantee you that it will be easier than if you had no map at all. Just as a real map guides you through unfamiliar landscapes, understanding the emotional phases will give you a context for what you are feeling. You will also be reassured to know that as long as you practice some self-care techniques, you will eventually arrive at a better destination. Parents who don't understand or acknowledge their own emotional journey end up having a much harder time, as was the case with Betty and Bob.

Betty's ideal child was someone who would share her and her husband's love of the sand and surf. She grew up in a small town near the ocean, and her favorite childhood memories were of being at the beach, in the family boat, surfing, and having picnics in the sand. She married Bob, a lawyer who was an avid surfer in his off hours. When Betty was pregnant, she and Bob joked about how soon they could put their baby on a surfboard. Betty couldn't wait to take her infant to the beach. Even her baby shower had a surf theme, with little blue surfboards on each table.

DEFINITION: OBSESSIVE-COMPULSIVE DISORDER

Obsessive-compulsive disorder (OCD) is a disorder of thinking and behavior that includes recurring obsessions, compulsive behaviors and repetitive actions that significantly impair a person's function. The current treatments that are most prevalent are cognitive behavior therapy and some medications.

But Tony was very different from the child Betty had imagined she would have. He had sensory problems as a toddler. He was touch-aversive and hated getting dirty. He despised the feeling of sand on his feet and preferred to stay inside watching TV. When he was six years old, his parents received his diagnosis: Tony had obsessive-compulsive disorder (OCD). Betty and Bob were given a list of interventions to follow for their son, recommendations that have been known to help children like Tony. Although they were completely overwhelmed, they bravely took on their new regimen: psychiatrist for medication, therapy once weekly for OCD, occupational therapy twice weekly for sensory coordination issues, and later, an educational therapist for learning strategies.

Betty and Bob coped with the regimen, but this was a very different life than the one they had imagined. Instead of spending leisurely days on the beach building sand castles with her son and later teaching him how to ride the waves, Betty was now in the car most afternoons, delivering Tony to his specialists. During his off time, her son just wanted to watch TV. Tony's therapist said that was okay because he needed to relax.

But what about Betty's fantasy of her beach baby? The son who would follow in his surfer dad's footsteps? How did she deal with giving up the family life she had envisioned? And how did she cope with her feelings about losing her ideal boy?

Without the necessary guidance about how to confront her

emotions, Betty became depressed. Her psychiatrist's response was to prescribe antidepressants. Although the medication helped her function more normally in her day-to-day life, her emotional world stayed flattened and her real feelings of loss for her "beach baby" stayed repressed.

Not all parents will go through depression as Betty did, but most will experience emotional challenges when their expectations deviate from the reality of who their child is. I offer Betty's story as a way to encourage you to confront your own feelings, beginning with those you had—or still have—about your ideal child.

Betty and Bob eventually moved to be closer to her parents. I wish I could have continued to work with them, and that I had the chance to offer Betty some perspective on how atypical children grow and evolve. Parents of these kids truly cannot imagine the variety of outcomes that are possible for their children. A rosy future can be very hard to fathom when you are driving your child to his third therapy appointment of the week. But I have known hundreds of children for ten or twenty years or longer, and I can assure you that whatever you think is going to happen with your child, it's probably not going to be what you envision when you are depressed, over-whelmed, or anxious. That is the upside of expectations: your worst-case scenario may very well be exaggerated, just as your ideal child was. That's how it was for Declan and his parents.

Declan: Freedom Is Knowing Yourself

I first started seeing Declan when he was seven years old. With au-burn hair and large green eyes, his looks were charming, but his af-fect was flat. He was behaviorally rigid, and while he wasn't depressed, neither was he expressing spontaneity or joy. Declan's language skills were above average; he was bright and able to learn his academics, but he had little social awareness. His mental flexibility was not devel-

---

DEFINITION: AUTISM SPECTRUM DISORDER

Autism spectrum disorder (ASD) is a general term for a developmental brain-based disorder. It is not a single diagnosis with a uniform profile. It is a spectrum of behaviors that are characterized by difficulties in social interactions. Those on the more severe end of the spectrum are nonverbal and are highly sensitive to sensory overload. They also have obsessive interests and behavioral compulsions. High-functioning children can be highly verbal with limited ability to navigate social relationships. The former term *Asperger syndrome* referred to those on the high-functioning end of the spectrum.

---

oped, so it was hard for him to make friends or solve problems. He was having meltdowns at home because the stimuli at school had started to overwhelm him.

Declan's parents were completely flummoxed about what to do with him. They didn't understand and they didn't want to understand, because their other kids were fine and they knew Declan was smart. In what I had come to recognize as a standard parental response, Dad was angry—*Why doesn't he just act normal?*—and Mom was overprotective. More than anything, they were confused.

My assessment of Declan came as an utter shock to his parents: Their son had high-functioning autism.

The diagnosis was devastating to them, but I explained that because Declan was high functioning, he might possibly evolve out of the diagnosis as long as he had strong parental support and the appropriate interventions. The concept of evolving out of autism is controversial, but I have seen children do it, and there is now research supporting this phenomenon.[5] The same day I gave Declan's parents his diagnosis, I also told them about places they could go for the guidance and services they would need to help Declan both academically and socially.

I continued to see Declan every few years, as his parents brought him in to be reassessed for progress. Most recently, he and his mom came to see me right before he entered college. Declan walked in and gave me a shy (spontaneous) smile. He spoke quietly about his experiences in senior year of high school and what he was looking forward to as a college freshman. He had developed his social skills to the point where he was accepted in his community, he had a small circle of friends, and he and his parents were getting along well. Academically Declan did need some accommodations, because he still required extra time for test-taking. But compared to where he was at age seven, this was a tremendous improvement. He didn't have a girlfriend—yet. That would probably be the last thing to develop, and he didn't have a clue how to go about it. (Then again, a lot of eighteen-year-old boys don't have a clue!)

Before they left, I pulled Declan's mother aside and together we reflected on how far Declan had come and what an amazing journey it had been.

"I'm so proud of him," she said. "He's an inspiration to me. I rely on his good common sense. He doesn't get rattled; he has kind of a soothing effect on me and the rest of the family."

What was originally observed as mental rigidity had evolved into mature problem-solving. Declan was that rare person who is truly objective and honest, so his mom greatly valued his opinion. What had been his flat affect and lack of emotional spontaneity now helped him, as he did not go through the jitters and anxiety that tormented most high school seniors. When it came to college, he simply reasoned: *If I study and get good grades, I'll go to college.* He was sanguine, calm. "He's kind of Zen-like," his mother said.

Declan understood that what could shatter his calm, Zen-like state was losing control, so he applied to colleges that would fit his needs. He knew he would be happiest and do best at a small college that offered dorms where he would be able to cook his own meals and could have his own room, with no roommate. Small class size would also be important. It wasn't hard to find numerous colleges that met those criteria.

"Declan's dad is proud of him too. He got straight A's in his junior and senior years," his mom said. Declan had attended a small high school—not a special-needs school, just a school that accepted different kinds of minds. The teachers gave him the support and encouragement he needed, and he got excellent grades. He would be going into engineering, which is common for people with autism. And off he went to college, launched!

Declan's progress had been slow but steady, and his parents had evolved along with him. Once they were acclimated to the idea of Declan having autism, they made sure he got the support he needed. They didn't have to wait for a college letter of acceptance to realize that their son would be able to appreciate and contribute to the world. Declan's rigidity turned out to be an asset, helping him pursue what he was passionate about. It turned into tenacity.

Have faith in yourself, have faith in your child, and keep an open heart and mind. You cannot know what your child's future will hold. Now, let's consider your own ideal child, so you can acknowledge the phantom and begin to let it go.

Reflecting on Your Idealized Child

Can you recall when you first started thinking about having a child?

- What—or rather, who—came to mind when you imagined what your child would be like? What did you imagine he or she would look like?
- What influences contributed to your image of the child you would one day parent? What did you think his or her personality would reflect?

- What attributes, strengths, and proclivities did you envision your child would have?
- How did you imagine your child would be similar or different from you? From your spouse or partner?
- How did you assume you would feel toward your ideal child?
- What feelings would he or she bring out in you?

As you think about these questions, notice feelings that come up for you. It might be difficult to acknowledge that you had expectations of what your child would be like, expectations that differ starkly from how your child actually is. You might be battling feelings of guilt or remorse for consciously bringing up this topic. I realize that it is a loaded subject, the idea of imagining a child who is different from the child you actually have. If this is difficult, don't force the issue, but just be aware that there are some deep feelings there.

When you have a fairly clear picture in your mind of your idealized child, take some time to acknowledge her or his presence in your thoughts. This imaginary child is who you hoped for and, to some extent, who you expected. Recognize that you conjured this image from various influences in your own life. Perhaps your fantasy child was an unreal projection of parts of yourself that you feel need completing or enhancing. Maybe your parents' expectations helped shape the image of your ideal child. Our culture's emphasis on success and perfection might have had an impact. By closely observing that image, you will be able to distinguish between your imaginary child and your real daughter or son. The ultimate objective, which we will work on throughout the book, is to let go of the idealized image of who your child was supposed to be. Shedding your conscious or unconscious expectations will free you to be more open to the variety in human behavior, recognizing that none of us is ideal, that no human being is without human imperfections.

It is not the imperfections that create difficulties, it is our expectations. Expectations make it so much harder for us to fully embrace both our children and ourselves. Ora, a deeply religious woman, was the mother of Natalie, a severely ill toddler born with an incurable terminal disease. Ora was a trained hospice care worker, which gave her a different perspective than that of most parents. She wisely observed, "Imagine if infants were born ready to use the potty and diapering wasn't in the norm of our expectations. If you gave birth to a baby who needed diapers, it would be considered a tragedy. The fact that you would have to change diapers for the first two years of life would be seen as a devastating concept. But every parent is able to change their babies' diapers. Why? Because it is the natural state of affairs."

Ora attributed her calm acceptance of her daughter's illness to her ability to let go of expectations and her own ego. She's right: The two are connected. When your child has a huge temper tantrum over getting his hands dirty, like Tony, or cannot enjoy a birthday party because she can't handle the sensory overload, does your ego take a bashing? Notice where this is coming from. Has your ideal image of your child—and of yourself as a parent—been battered? Do you leave upset and embarrassed? And does that embarrassment lead to anger at home, to crying or feelings of deep disappointment later that night, as you relive what your friends must be thinking about you, or worry about how your child is not going to be able to make any friends? If so, being aware is the first step to changing your expectations and accepting the real world.

> It is not the imperfections that create difficulties, it is our expectations.

Priming Yourself for Parenting Your Real (Not Ideal) Child

Parents of atypical kids are trained to prime their children before sending them to activities that may be overstimulating or otherwise upsetting. They rehearse the upcoming event: "This is what's going to happen. There will be a lot of kids. If you get nervous, here's what you're going to do." But parents don't prime themselves. How are you going to feel when your child freaks out in front of all your friends? How are you going to handle your embarrassment?

The best way to make a plan for success is to study the past and prepare for the future. Think back to the last disastrous event with your atypical child. Here is an example using the mother of an eight-year-old son with sensory processing disorder and high-functioning autism:

1. What was the situation?
2. How did you react in the moment?
3. How did that work for you?
4. What can you learn from that?
5. What do you need to do next time in order to avoid a repetition of this event?

When you carefully observe your behavior, you might feel defensive or embarrassed about what you are writing down. I encourage

---

DEFINITION: SENSORY PROCESSING DISORDER

Sensory processing disorder is not a diagnosis in the traditional diagnostic categories, and there are some clinicians who believe that it is part of a developmental pattern consistent with autism or an underlying medical condition. It is believed to be a condition in which the brain has trouble receiving and responding to information that comes in through the senses, such as being oversensitive to sounds, lights, or touch. It also implies difficulties in coordination and processing some types of information. Sensory processing disorder is not currently recognized as a standalone disorder by psychologists and psychiatrists. It is mostly treated by occupational therapists.

1. What was the situation?	Jon fell apart at the neighborhood birthday party because he was overstimulated.
2. How did you react in the moment?	I grabbed Jon and ran home mortified.
3. How did that work out for you?	We did not stay long enough to try to help Jon cope with the stimulation because I was too embarrassed in front of the other parents.
4. What did you learn from this experience?	I need to emotionally prepare myself to handle Jon's unpredictable outbursts and not pay attention to others. I can help him if I am prepared.
5. What can you do next time to prepare?	Prepare myself emotionally. Put Jon first. Let go of my expectations. Focus on what is really important: helping Jon. I can only do this if I am cognizant of my feelings and let go of my expectations that Jon will have typical reactions. Whatever comes, I will accept and deal with it.

you to keep a chart like this and to use compassion and humor in recording your daily episodes and responses. Let it be okay if you didn't handle events perfectly. Of course things don't always run smoothly. We're human. You deserve just as much compassion as you feel toward your child. As you work to accept yourself, you will be training your brain and emotions to be more resilient, empathetic, and flexible. If you regularly write down these events, especially after reading this book, you will be able to chart your progress from fear to confidence, anger to acceptance.

Sylvia Boorstein, a noted Buddhist teacher, uses these phrases to soothe and encourage people who are struggling: *May you be well. May you be cared for. May you be joyful.* As you continue on this journey, I will help you move toward greater acceptance of yourself, your child, and those around you. In the meantime, may you be well, may you be cared for, may you be joyful.

CHAPTER TWO

The Denial Phase

"Not My Child!"

*I knew there was something different about Carlo, but my husband
kept brushing off everything I told him, as if I were making a big
deal out of nothing. "You're just being neurotic," he'd say. "I used to
act weird like that when I was little too." But why would a five-year-
old be so obsessed with an old-fashioned record player? All Carlo
wanted to do was watch a record go around and around, instead of
playing with other kids. Michael just couldn't admit that Carlo was
very different from other children his age.*

— Allegra, mother of a five-year-old with autism spectrum disorder

• • •

As parents become aware of their children's unique challenges,
they find themselves on a journey that often begins with that
first inkling that something is not quite right. Allegra had that worried sense about Carlo, but her husband clearly did not. She was
concerned about Carlo's odd behavior, whereas Michael felt their son
was perfectly fine. Three years into parenting together, they were
interpreting events differently.

All parents are on a journey that begins before their child's birth,
when they imagine their future as a family, and continues as they
guide their child through the many stages of his or her development.

If your child is atypical, the journey expands to include learning about your son or daughter's strengths and differences and making important decisions about treatments and care. You wade through uncertainty as you rely on your parental instincts and the advice of trusted professionals. You realize that getting a diagnosis and plugging in the appropriate remediation is only part of what will be required of you as a caring parent. Circumstances change, the family dynamic changes, and your child changes as well. The truth about raising any child is that the experience is filled with unexpected twists and turns, both confounding and delightful.

Like Allegra, you may find that one of the first unanticipated twists is your partner's refusal to acknowledge that something is going on with your child. Instead, your parenting partner may believe that everything is just fine and be in denial about certain aspects of your child's behavior. Or *you* may be the denying parent. So let's define our terms. What exactly is denial, and is it necessarily a bad thing?

> *The human mind isn't a terribly logical or consistent place. Most people, given the choice to face a hideous or terrifying truth or to conveniently avoid it, choose the convenience and peace of normality. That doesn't make them strong or weak people, or good or bad people. It just makes them people.*
>
> —Jim Butcher, *Turn Coat*

Denial Is There to Protect Us

Denial is a healthy response to hearing for the first time that your child may have an unexpected condition. It protects you from feelings that initially may be too upsetting or threatening. Finding out that your son or daughter may be different enough to require special treatment can definitely be a shock to your system, so flinching from this reality is understandable. Denial temporarily protects you from tumultuous emotions.

Denial is a *defense mechanism*, a term coined by Sigmund Freud. It is, in part, an unconscious psychological strategy designed to help us manage anxiety. In neuropsychological terms, defense mechanisms create a homeostasis, or balance, in our brain so that we can cope with stress and stay fully functional. If we were to let our distressing emotions overwhelm our cognitive reasoning, we would become emotionally paralyzed and unable to carry on with our lives. We would become part of a fairly large group of folks I refer to as the worriers.

We all know people who worry all the time. Maybe you are one of them. Worriers are people who are unable to find a balance between their emotions and their reasoning (what the experts call "healthy emotional homeostasis"). They do not have a system of denial in place; instead, their worry radar is always targeting potential dangers: *My baby will catch a cold in this rainy weather . . . She might fall if I let her walk down the steps by herself . . . If I let him play with the neighbor's kids, he'll learn bad habits . . . The ingredients in this toothpaste could be terribly harmful . . .* and so on. All parents know that their worry radar can remain overactive regardless of their child's age. As a matter of fact, there are some people who are simply too worry-prone to have children at all, people who think: *I can't imagine bringing children into this toxic, violent, dangerous world.* Of course, their fears are not without some truth. We do live in a world with a multitude of dangers, most of which we have absolutely no control over.

The fact that many of us have children despite the dangers proves an important point: It takes courage to bring a child into our troubled world, and that courage requires a certain level of denial. If we think too intently about war, hunger, violence, environmental hazards, prejudice, the economy, or nuclear threat, how would we ever make the decision to have a child? Our ability to store these concerns in the back of our minds when we decide to become parents—our healthy level of denial—enables us to move forward with our lives and usher in the next generation. For this purpose, denial is a wonderful thing. It protects us from over-worrying about the potential dangers that might befall our children.

Denial protects us as well from becoming overwhelmed by the information that our child might have a serious problem. It enables us to carry on and not go into panic mode when a spouse, teacher, or psychologist first brings up the possibility of a developmental issue or other condition. Denying that this is a valid possibility is perfectly okay—initially. It simply means that you (or your partner) are protecting yourself against panic and emotional upheaval.

A parent's initial denial also reflects a very positive attribute—optimism—which is absolutely essential if a child is to grow up with a confident, upbeat outlook. When you become a parent, you become your child's primary cheerleader. If you don't believe in your heart that your child is the greatest, your optimistically oriented denial system is not working and you become too critical. In this sense, denial is a beneficial trait, and when I see it in my clients I am touched by their parental love and positive outlook.

I commend a parent's denial on this level. I appreciate parents who come into my office and tell me how incredible their kid is. Their unconditional love and enthusiastic testimony on their child's behalf is inspiring. I share that enthusiasm and convey to them that I want to be their kid's champion too. Although my role as a neuropsychologist is to identify atypical conditions and behaviors so that children can receive the attention they need, I also want to be the child's advocate along with his or her parents. Every child is vulnerable, and if we're not their fans, who will be?

I believe that optimism can be at the root of a parent's denial, and that is heartening to me as a psychologist, a mom, and someone who cares deeply about children. Optimistic denial is healthy denial, as is the initial denial that protects you from the upsetting news that your child may have a disorder that could impact his or her future. It is only when a parent's denial lasts for months or years, preventing the parent from taking necessary steps to help the child, that it veers from healthy to dysfunctional.

> *Hope is the denial of reality.*
>
> —Margaret Weis, fantasy novelist

A Common Version of Denial: "I Was Just like Him When I Was a Kid!"

In the case of Michael, the dad in the vignette that opened this chapter, years went by before he was able to break through his denial and acknowledge that his wife, Allegra, had been on to something when their son was only two. Allegra had felt uneasy about little Carlo during their third or fourth mommy-and-me class. In previous classes, Carlo had wandered off on his own, completely disinterested in the planned activities, playing instead with a brightly colored set of plastic toy keys that Allegra kept in her bag. Allegra had ignored his behavior at first, because Carlo was neither disruptive nor unhappy. But at this particular class, not only was Carlo not interested in playing with the other children or getting involved with the various activities the other moms and kids were engaged in, he was completely preoccupied with the padlock on a cabinet in the room where the class was being held. Carlo was so mesmerized by the lock that he played with it for the entire hour. While the other kids were singing and clapping and sitting on their mom's laps, Carlo was fiddling with the padlock, clanking it this way and that, ignoring everything else.

That night at dinner, Allegra mentioned to Michael what had occurred in class that day. "I'm kind of worried that Carlo is so unsocial, so oblivious to everything that's going on," she said. "And the way he was obsessed with that padlock was really odd." Allegra's worry radar was beeping like crazy, but Michael was unconcerned. "Are you sure? Maybe he's just more into mechanical stuff than singing songs."

Allegra held her ground. "I just have this feeling something might be wrong."

Michael felt his stomach clench. He held his breath and thought for a moment. He looked at his upset wife and his adorable son, who was playing with his SpaghettiOs. Then he shook his head as if to brush the worry from his mind and said, "No, you're wrong. Everything is fine."

But Carlo continued to have unusual obsessions. He went from padlocks to watching records spin around and around on his parents' old-fashioned phonograph. He was not at all interested in playing with other children, and the only time he would tolerate a playdate was if the other kid agreed to share his fascination with the spinning records. Carlo's rigid interests and lack of sociability continued to worry Allegra, so she finally talked to her pediatrician about her son's behavior. The doctor's response was very similar to Michael's. "Don't worry. Kids go through phases," Carlo's doctor told her. "Besides, your son is so bright. You have nothing to be concerned about."

It was true that Carlo was exceptionally bright, as evidenced on the first day of preschool when he was three. He walked into the classroom, looked up at the door and asked Allegra, "Where's the exit sign that should usually go there?" Needless to say, most three-year-olds don't read the word *exit*, nor are they as keenly observant as little Carlo was. Because he was such an intelligent child, everyone except Allegra was in denial about how odd certain of his behaviors were. Although he appeared cheerful, Carlo didn't make friends in preschool. When the other kids engaged in group play, Carlo would play by himself, off in his own world. Allegra had noticed this on the several occasions when she volunteered in his class, but there were no reports sent home to her and Michael warning them that something was amiss in Carlo's socialization skills.

It wasn't until Carlo reached kindergarten that his teachers noticed he was becoming increasingly robotic and continued to be obsessed with certain things, including the San Francisco Bay Area Rapid Transit (BART) system. He could recite by heart all the BART stops in the city, where his family had visited, and he would offer this information to whomever would listen. Further, during recess Carlo would stand in the playground shouting out stops on the BART line rather than playing. At home he was not progressing in his self-help skills and continued to need much supervision with basic hygiene. Finally the school principal notified Allegra and Michael that Carlo's behavior seemed highly unusual and that perhaps they should have him tested.

Of course, Allegra had suspected that there was something strange about Carlo's behavior ever since those early experiences in mommy-and-me class. But while she had been aware of a potential problem for years, Michael continued to deny that anything was wrong. It is very common for one parent to suspect that something is troubling or different about their child, while the other parent disagrees. Allegra contended that they needed to see a professional to check out what the school official had reported, but Michael again pushed back. "There's absolutely nothing the matter with Carlo! I was just like that when I was his age—ask my mother. I'm fine, and he'll grow up to be fine too."

Allegra could not understand why the reports from the principal and other "hard evidence," as she put it, failed to move her husband. The research of Bessel A. van der Kolk, a pioneer in the field of trauma and its impact, sheds some light on Michael's reactions. Van der Kolk found that feeling threatened hinders a person's ability to process verbal communication or to reason about the perceived threat.

Yet on a sensory level, the truth may be sinking in. The results shows up in physical symptoms such as insomnia, loss of appetite, headaches, stomachaches, and many more.

> *The mind doesn't seem to be particularly well-equipped to entirely abolish unacceptable emotions, thoughts or impulses. In fact, it seems more geared to creating a rationale for troublesome behavior instead of eliminating it.*
>
> —Bessel A. van der Kolk, pioneering researcher,
> author, and expert on traumatic stress

As an aside, I'd like to mention here a technique we'll be talking about in later chapters: the power of physical touch to release oxytocin, a hormone that calms anxiety. As counterintuitive as it may seem while you're presenting "hard evidence" to a denying partner, what actually might work better is a hug. The denier is frightened and has shut down. Had Allegra been able to give Michael a long hug and say, "We're in this together. We'll make it work," her words and touch would have released oxytocin, which might have softened Michael's wall of resistance. Pat Ogden referred to this as working "from the bottom up," that is, from your body and physical sensations to regain control of your cognitive brain.[1] You can use inner body sensation to calm someone close to you through hugging, or if you're a clinician trying to calm anxious parents, through a reassuring pat on the shoulder or a handshake. Softening a person's resistance can be more effective than trying to break through it with hard cognitive evidence.

The Body Knows the Truth

Michael's denial had lasted for three years at this point. But it's easy to be in denial for years when you go to work all week and don't see your child's behavior on a day-in, day-out basis. What sometimes happens is that an event such as a birthday party breaks partway through the denial. The less involved parent might take the child to a party, see with his own eyes how very different the child's behavior is, and think to himself (it's too scary to acknowledge it out loud), *Oh my god . . .* and just leave it at that. Michael may have had such experiences with Carlo. But the story he was able to tell himself was, "I was just like him when I was a boy." Meanwhile, Michael was losing his appetite and his stomach was constantly in knots. At work, it was getting hard to concentrate. Rationalize though he might, the truth was getting closer, and Michael's body knew it even if Michael was not yet ready to consciously accept it.

Stress feeds denial, and another factor that likely contributed to Michael's denial was his stressful life. Like most parents with young kids, his schedule was hectic and demanding. Denying that anything was wrong with Carlo enabled Michael to carry on with the myriad activities that comprised his normal routine. People who are already overstressed may resist change because they sense it will only add more anxiety and expense to their lives.

It is part of our psychological makeup to want to maintain our balance (homeostasis). We like our routines because they allow us to follow the expected path we set forth for ourselves. Routines are calming. For Michael, the path he expected for his son was: *Carlo will complete preschool. He will enroll in public kindergarten and elementary school, where he will do well. In high school, maybe he'll be on the track team, like I was—he's got the legs for it! He'll graduate high school and move on to a good college. Thank God we have twelve years to save for that.*

If Michael had to alter this schedule and insert the steps required to address a problem with Carlo's behavior, it would cause him to veer off into an unknown direction. So there was a lot of resistance to hearing that such a problem was a possibility. Instead: *There's nothing wrong with Carlo. Don't mess up the plan.*

Diagnosis Day

As the reality of Carlo's condition became harder to deny, Michael edged closer to dealing with it. Back in the principal's office a week later, he said, "I still don't think anything's wrong, but I don't want to be the bad guy." He grudgingly agreed to allow Carlo to be tested, all the while feeling very nervous about it. Allegra was equally nervous, but her desire get to the bottom of the problem propelled her forward. She brought Carlo to three sessions with a neuropsychologist and a meeting was set up to discuss the results.

The day of the meeting arrived after a sleepless night for both of them. "What if we hear really bad news?" Allegra whispered. "Somehow we'll get through it," Michael replied, but inside, he wasn't so sure.

At the neuropsychologist's office, they were told about Carlo's strengths. The couple was gratified to learn that Carlo was indeed quite bright. In fact, he fell into the gifted category of children in terms of his IQ, particularly in his verbal skills. Michael's stomach relaxed and he leaned back, feeling more confident, until the neuropsychologist began to address Carlo's problematic behaviors and social and emotional development.

Michael doesn't have a good recollection of what happened next. There was a lot of buzzing in his head, and he remembers hearing the words *autism spectrum disorder* and *very high functioning*—or did he make up the word *very*? Michael and Allegra both went on autopilot. He vaguely remembers shaking the psychologist's hand and walking out of the office, but he can't recall how he got home. The report sat on their desk for a week. There was no conversation about it. Michael couldn't bear to look at it.

What Does It Feel Like to Be in Denial?

Michael's story gives us an idea of how a parent may react when he is in denial about his child's possible differences. By the time he and Allegra met with the school principal, Michael's body was already processing the truth about Carlo by disrupting Michael's sleep, ruining his appetite, and causing stomach pains. His physical reactions in the psychologist's office were typical of the "deer in the headlights" freeze response to traumatic news.

When you have an unconscious resistance to change, much of this resistance is registered on a physiological level. Very often the first response to hearing news you don't like is a feeling of numbness, which is similar to what you feel when you undergo any type of traumatic experience. During the traumatic incident and for a certain amount of time afterward, you become incapable of processing information in a rational way. Just like in many mammalian species, "playing dead" until the perceived threat has passed is a human survival strategy. Your reasoning brain and emotional brain both go into a kind of temporary hibernation while your lower brain systems (known as the reptilian brain or brainstem) take over. These enable you to function by relying on your automatic memory rather than making conscious decisions. People refer to this as going on "automatic" or "autopilot." Being on autopilot allows the body to go through the motions of daily living without having to process thoughts or feelings.

Many people who feel externally threatened by upsetting news about their children will initially shut down, go into withdrawal, and slow down their emotional reactions. People have told me, "When I first heard the news about our child, I went numb. I was on autopilot for the rest of the day, going through my daily routine but unable to think, feel, or make decisions." These parents are temporarily immobilized.

In neuropsychological theory, being on automatic is referred to as the *freeze response*, indicating that a threat has been noted and the response is one of "alert immobility."[2] Freezing involves a range of reactions that can be as simple as emotionally freezing up (feeling numb or going on autopilot) to a physical behavior that allows you to flee from the situation (such as getting into bed and watching reruns all day, in order to withdraw from reality and gain emotional balance by shutting down and doing something comforting). In other words, freezing involves an inhibition of motor activity and little emotional reactivity. In neuropsychological terms, both your neocortex (decision making abilities) and your limbic system (your emotional regulator) hibernate in the face of perceived danger. During this state, the underlying emotion is mild fear or anxiety. It includes behavioral changes such as increased heart rate, decreased salivation, respiratory changes, increased startle response, and difficulty speaking.[3]

When you come to an abrupt stop, freeze all your movements, and hold your breath, even language is inhibited. The freeze response can also impact memory formation during that time period and temporarily inhibit your ability to express yourself.[4] Parents can become so shut down during a meeting with a teacher or doctor that they are unable to articulate their thoughts or remember exactly what was said. This is not conscious avoidance or resistance; it is a normal reaction to stressful news.

A typical comment I hear from parents who are in denial is, "I'm only here because the school told us they won't take our child unless we get him tested." Such parents usually have expressions of wide-eyed alarm and stay very quiet in the interview session. I interpret their quietness as numbness. They are in shock that their child has been singled out as different. It's a horrible feeling for parents to think of their child as anything less than absolutely fine and perfectly normal, which is why I have a great deal of empathy for parents who are in denial. Unfortunately, they are usually unable to feel my empathy because the news is too new. They are shut down emotionally, and I understand that.

Why Is It So Hard to Change?
The Neurobiology of Denial

Often, the feeling associated with denial is resistance. Resistance is not a voluntary response. Our neuronal connections are responsible for this reaction to new information. Whenever you have a new idea and that idea leads to a new action, a set of neurons wire together at the synapses. Those connections create a "groove" in your brain called a *synaptic connection*. The more frequently an idea leads to the same action, the deeper the groove, and the more intense the synaptic connection. This phenomenon is called the Hebbian principle: *Neurons that fire together wire together.*

The adult brain has lots of these synaptic connections—fixed neuronal patterns that make up our habitual behaviors. Because of these well-worn connections, it is hard for us to change many of our behaviors. When a new synaptic connection is introduced—such as learning a new way to swing your tennis racket—the synaptic connectivity adapts in order to accommodate this new behavior. It may take many practice sessions to make this new swing more automatic. The ease with which you can change an old pattern and replace or add a new pattern depends on the brain's neuroplasticity. The more plastic (flexible) the brain, the more easily it adapts to a new concept.

Some people's lives seem to flow in a narrative; mine had many stops and starts. That's what trauma does. It interrupts the plot. You can't process it because it doesn't fit with what came before or what comes afterward. A friend of mine, a soldier, put it this way. In most of our lives, most of the time, you have a sense of what is to come. There is a steady narrative, a feeling of "lights, camera, action" when big events are imminent. But trauma isn't

like that. It just happens, and then life goes on. No one prepares
you for it.

—Jessica Stern, *Denial: A Memoir of Terror*

Children's brains are exceptionally plastic because their neuronal connections are fresh and unformed. If a child has a problem, he or she learns to deal with it by trying different solutions. Although recent popular books tout the neuroplasticity of mature brains, I find that claim somewhat exaggerated. In general, our mature brains tend to rebel against change and cling to our habits. It takes more work to change when you are older. It's especially wrenching to change established beliefs such as "I'm a good person and a good parent, therefore my child is going to be well-adjusted and successful."

The neuropsychology behind a parent's denial boils down to resistance that is due to our wiring: *Don't knock me off my program. I am not willing to consider change right now. My child is doing fine. I don't accept that there is something wrong.* Whatever your habitual thinking pattern, it is extremely hard to get in there and adjust it. That doesn't mean it can't be done. In fact, altering our thinking in order to benefit our children is part of healthy parenting, and we can consciously make the effort to promote our brain's neuroplasticity. This involves adapting to new, incoming information, such as a child's diagnosis, and saying, "Okay, now what do we do?" Transforming yourself from a denying parent into a resilient parent who can say, "Let's go for it!" is what this book is all about.

"I'm the Only One Who Understands My Child"

There is another issue that often is associated with parents' denial of their child's learning difference: the desire for perfection. This happens when our best wishes for our child and societal and media hype reinforce each other. Parents are led to believe that if they read all the best baby books, buy all the right toys, provide the right types of enrichment, and engage in the right type of attachment parenting style, their child is going to be perfect—or at the very least, ahead of the curve. I have heard parents note with pride that when it came to academic milestones, their child was far ahead of the game compared to others in the class . . . in kindergarten!

Such over-the-top parental pride can be seen as a type of culturally induced mindset, fueled by a generation of highly educated parents and a thriving industry devoted to child-development materials. In a sense, parents are led into thinking that their child's future success in life is utterly contingent upon how well a parent oversees and manages his or her child's every waking moment. The spike in child-rearing theories and the availability of infinite online information has led parents to believe that with enough effort on their part, they can single-handedly push their child over the finish line to "success."

Many loving parents, although well-meaning, see their children as extensions of themselves. Their children must represent them in ways that meet the parents' emotional needs. How does such over-identification influence a parent's denial? The more invested someone is, the less able he or she is to absorb information from others. If a child's diagnosis doesn't compute in the overidentified parent's brain, the diagnosis doesn't exist. I often hear such a parent say, "I'm the only one who really knows what my child is like." Or "I'm so plugged into my child, and you just don't understand him." Or "My child has a very unique way of looking at the world, and other people sometimes can't understand that."

I'm not dismissing a parent's feeling that his or her child is singularly delightful and amazing. I feel that way about my own children. However, the word *unique* is sometimes used by a parent to deny the child's need for treatment or remediation, and it then becomes an impediment to that child's well-being and success in life. While we can honor all children's uniqueness, we must also honor the struggles they are going through and do whatever we can to address their needs.

The denial of some parents is so extreme that they won't even read a school's assessment report. Or they demand that the testing professional eliminate certain "incriminating information" from the report because "it doesn't sound like our child at all." After learning about the remediation process recommended for their child, they'll take the report and in a disengaged manner say, "Thank you very much." Then they will completely disregard it. Some parents refuse to follow up on even one of the recommendations. Some become so defensive that they genuinely believe they alone are capable of knowing what their child is like and what's best for him or her.

Parents such as these may feel as if the army is attacking their entire family. They go into retreat mode until they are marooned at the top of a hill in their castle with a moat around them, protecting their child from perceived threat. It's not unusual for these parents to take radical action, such as withdrawing their child from school and deciding to homeschool, or moving to another state. Their denial can propel them into irrational behaviors in response to what they have learned, without ever rationally addressing the information.

There can be a fine line between knowing your child, feeling close to your child, and not being able to see this child as he or she truly is because you're still looking through the lens of the perfect child fantasy. Brian was that type of parent. He was on his second marriage, with two grown children from his first. In his mid-fifties, Brian was anticipating a happy retirement in a plush golf village on the ocean, when his much younger wife gave birth to a little boy. Ashton was a lovely child, but reports of hyperactivity and difficulty with learning how to read had followed him since nursery school. He was already in third grade and wasn't yet reading or writing. But he could stand on his head, do handstands in my office, and had a beautiful smile. He was also the mirror image of Brian, who closely identified with him. In our meetings, Brian repeated the same refrain he had been using since Ashton's nursery school days: "He's exactly like me. I raised two other children who were also slow to read, and they are all grown up and doing fine. You just don't understand our family learning style."

Brian grudgingly agreed to get a tutor for Ashton but refused to consider more intensive interventions, such as medication treatment for ADHD or an intensive five-day-a-week program to treat his dyslexia. "I remember going to these teacher meetings with my older kids," he told me. "All you guys are the same, you don't get it. My kids turn out fine, you'll see."

Unfortunately, being in denial doesn't equate with being able to turn off your feelings. A few months later, Brian suffered a mild heart attack. He admitted that some of his anxiety came from trying to not think about Ashton's condition. His refusal to cope with negative emotions created a buildup of anxiety and stress in him. Brian began intensive psychotherapy aimed at stress reduction and lifestyle changes, including adjusting to the idea that his little boy needed more intervention than he had been willing to admit and that his retirement plans needed to be pushed back in order to accommodate this financial reality—not an easy list of changes to make. But slowly, over time, he was able to adapt. Today Ashton is thriving in a special-needs school, and Brian is close to his desired retirement.

"We Don't Believe in Psychology"

In some families, cultural bias and ingrained beliefs pose a serious obstacle to parents accepting a child's diagnosis. The parents' natural fear is exacerbated by the (sometimes valid) worry that having a child who is different will imperil their position in the community and maybe even cause them to be ostracized.

The members of Dev and Amari's community never openly discussed differences of any type. When their son, Naval, was in the second grade, his school reported that he was having difficulty sitting in his chair, listening to the teacher, and paying attention to what was going on in class. The principal referred Dev and Amari to me to have Naval tested. Although they would not on their own have sought out a psychologist for their son, they trusted the school's judgment.

Initially, Naval's parents were very cooperative. They answered my questions, talked to me about Naval's family life, agreed to the testing, brought Naval in for the tests, and were always courteous and respectful. But when it came time to discuss the diagnosis of their extremely hyperactive and anxious child, they began to protest. "Naval is a very nice boy," Amari said forcefully. "He is good to me. He is good to his little sister. He does his homework. I don't understand all these terminologies. Why are you trying to say my son is sick?"

Behind Dev and Amari's denial was a fear that Naval's diagnosis and treatment would change their family's status in their community. Among certain cultures and religious groups, differences are extremely taboo. It was clear that Amari and Dev were uncomfortable with my diagnosis and wanted to keep it under wraps. I understood their alarm, but at the same time there was a very real child here with a real problem—and an available solution, which would involve going to a therapist as well as interventions Dev and Amari could do at home.

Amari made it clear to me that taking her son to a therapist was unacceptable. In their community, such treatment would signal that their child "had problems" and would put a black mark on the whole family. She feared, somewhat justifiably, that there would be no more outings with other families, no more playdates, and no marriage proposals for Naval or any of his siblings.

Not only did Dev and Amari deny that I had accurately diagnosed their child, they also denied the value of psychology in general. They did not believe in giving their child diagnostic labels that identified his anxiety, hyperactivity, and learning struggles. Their denial

---

DEFINITION: ATTENTION-DEFICIT/HYPERACTIVITY DISORDER

Children and adults with Attention-Deficit/Hyperactivity Disorder (ADHD) show a persistent pattern of inattention and/or hyperactivity/impulsivity that significantly interferes with their functioning or development, observed in at least two different environments. Currently, the specific diagnostic categories include three types of ADHD: inattentive, hyperactive, or combined types.

---

was based on their reluctance to adjust their belief system because to do so threatened their cultural norms. I know how extremely difficult making such an adjustment can be, even if it means helping your child overcome a serious problem.

Amari and Dev's reactions to Naval's diagnosis diverged somewhat. Dev was a bit more open-minded, whereas Amari was exceptionally dogmatic. She had a particular worldview of how children are supposed to be raised, and she was adamant that Naval did not need treatment for ADHD—a condition she didn't really believe existed. I had many sessions with the couple in my office as well as at Naval's school, where the principal and Naval's teacher joined us. As we discussed Naval's situation together, Amari learned that there were other children in the school who had been diagnosed with ADHD and were being medicated as well as receiving therapy. She came to realize that neither the diagnosis nor the treatment of it were as rare—or as atrocious—as she had imagined. Slowly, with Dev's encouragement, she came around.

Time and education go a long way toward breaking through denial about your child's condition. In Dev and Amari's case, it took about a year to consent to the treatment that their son needed. That is not uncommon, and some parents take even longer. The sad part is that while the parents deny and drag their feet, their child could be getting help (and in some cases, getting help sooner rather than later is crucial).

Treatment made a huge difference in Naval's life. When I checked on him three years later, in fifth grade, he was doing extremely well in school. Both Amari and Dev were convinced they had made the right decision.

"But Look How Well He Reads!"

Occasionally a mother and father's love for their child results in denial of almost heroic proportions. In these situations, the denial has mushroomed into an alternate reality that blots out even the most obvious facts.

Scott and Brianna came to me for an assessment of their fourteen-year-old son, Danny. He was a twin who had been born with several neurodevelopmental conditions and had received numerous interventions since he was a toddler. They wanted an updated assessment for their son because his school refused to place him in a typical classroom.

Scott and Brianna described Danny as definitely smart enough to be mainstreamed. According to them, he was just "emotionally and socially immature." Before I met with Danny, I tended to agree with Scott and Brianna's condemnation of the school board. I wondered if Scott and Brianna had asked to have a shadow (a personal assistant in the classroom for a special-needs child) for Danny, and they told me that the school wouldn't allow the boy in a mainstream classroom even with a shadow. Something was definitely not right. I agreed to see Danny for an assessment.

When Danny walked into my office, he had the demeanor of a much younger child. With a broad grin on his face and glasses sliding down his nose, he greeted me enthusiastically. "Good morning, Dr.

DEFINITION: INTELLECTUAL DISABILITY

Intellectual disability is a disability characterized by significant limitations in both intellectual functioning and in adaptive behavior, which covers many everyday social and practical skills. This cannot be diagnosed by an IQ test alone but should include an appraisal of a person's adaptive behavior as well.

Rita!" he proclaimed jovially. As his mom led him into the room, she showed him where to sit and opened his drink for him. He sat obediently with a cheerful yet somewhat blank expression on his face. While we were doing the testing, Danny became mischievous, tickling me under the table several times and then pulling his hand back and saying, "I didn't do that, I didn't do that!"—like a four-year-old might.

After the testing it was clear to me that Danny met criteria for intellectual disability (mental retardation) as well as hyperactivity. The diagnosis for intellectual disability is based on more than an IQ score. It also takes into consideration the individual's adaptive functioning (what he or she is able to understand and communicate) and daily living skills (such as getting dressed, using the bathroom, and feeding oneself). Danny's IQ score placed him on the scale between mild and moderate retardation. His self-help skills were lacking, he spilled a lot, and he needed help with the simplest tasks, such as wiping his chocolate moustache off his face. Emotionally and socially, he was very childlike. His hyperactivity made him restless and mischievous. After assessing all these things, it was apparent that Danny clearly could not maintain age-appropriate behavioral standards in a typical classroom.

But there was one very surprising fact about Danny, which served as Scott and Brianna's "proof" that their son was fine: Danny was not only reading, he was reading *Lord of the Flies*! I was astonished that

Danny was reading such a sophisticated book. Of course, I didn't communicate my surprise to either Danny or his parents, but I did ask Danny if he would bring the book to our next session. When he appeared with the book the following week, I asked him to read a paragraph. Danny read the paragraph and was able to tell me, in a very immature way, but clearly, what the paragraph was about. How was it possible that someone who functioned at a cognitive level far below his age could communicate the meaning of a book such as *Lord of the Flies*? The answer could be found in his parents' level of denial.

Scott and Brianna were in denial about Danny's cognitive limitations, and they had worked remarkably hard to prove to themselves that their son was as smart as any other boy his age. Brianna had homeschooled Danny in the traditional school subjects as well as focusing on one particular book: *Lord of the Flies*. She and Danny read the book several times, watched the movie, and discussed it over and over. Scott and Brianna's belief was that with enough coaching, Danny could take on any challenge. This was a case of a passionately committed mother and father who were in an extremely optimistic type of denial.

Scott and Brianna's story brought home to me a bittersweet truth: Denial can be lovingly well intentioned yet not in the child's best interest. These well-meaning parents were insisting on sending their son to a typical school even though it was clear to everyone else that Danny would not survive in a mainstream school. Danny was not socially or intellectually able to interact with others in a normal school setting. He was dependent on his parents' constant assistance. How had Danny made it as far as he had? People who are intellectually challenged can learn how to read if you work with them, and Scott and Brianna had worked intensely with Danny. They had devoted their lives to their son, and at fourteen years old, Danny was doing well for someone with his limitations. But Scott and Brianna could not always be the intellectual buffers between Danny and the outside world.

Although this is an unusual case, I cite it in order to demonstrate that denial can be the driving force behind the fight against limitations. This type of denial is positive and inspiring, as long as it doesn't prevent parents from getting the most appropriate treatment or school situation for their children. Danny needed to be in an environment where he could learn to thrive on his own without being constantly propped up by his parents.

It took a number of meetings with Scott and Brianna for them to acknowledge that Danny's learning differences required special attention in a setting tailored to his needs. I complimented them on the work they had done with their son, while also making clear that Danny would benefit immensely from the education he would receive from a specialized placement. Like all parents in the throes of denial, Scott and Brianna needed time and education to break through their reluctance to see their son in a more realistic light. At the same time, their story highlights some of the amazing things that extraordinary parents do for their kids. I feel honored to have known them.

"Just a Mild Case, No Big Deal"

Sometimes denial is an unconscious group agreement. When a child looks and acts typically, it can be hard to imagine that there might be something wrong. I call dyslexia "the invisible disorder" because it often appears, with no warning, in otherwise typically developing children. Parents, teachers, and even pediatricians have a tendency to give a child with a reading delay "the gift of time," reasoning that all children develop at their own pace. It's true that some kids read by age four, whereas others aren't reading until age seven or later. It is also true that the offices of pediatricians and school principals are flooded with anxious parents, many of whom have nothing to worry about. As a result, *all* concerned parents are generally given a pat on the back and told to be patient. There evolves an entire network of people who are in denial about certain children's inability to progress academically. That was the case with Isobel.

Isobel's difficulty learning to read began in preschool. Her teachers told her parents, Samantha and Ian, that their daughter was having a hard time learning her letters and writing her name. Mom and Dad didn't pay much attention. "Preschool is mainly about getting along with other kids," Samantha told herself. "Besides, I didn't learn my letters until kindergarten, so what's the big rush? I don't want to be a helicopter parent who jumps on every little thing." Isobel's teacher allowed the girl to advance to the next level but told Samantha and Ian to keep an eye on her progress. Their pediatrician agreed that it was too early to worry.

Isobel didn't make much progress in kindergarten either; she was still struggling. So in the summer between kindergarten and first grade, the kindergarten teacher recommended that Samantha and Ian hire Isobel's future first-grade teacher as a tutor. This arrangement is a very common one for children who are behind in their "reading readiness" prior to entering first grade. Isobel's parents went along with the program and hired the tutor for weekly support.

By first grade it did not appear that the tutoring had made a significant impact. Isobel couldn't sound out her letters, write her name consistently, or say the alphabet without singing it. She was flipping her *b*'s and *d*'s and had a lot of confusion when trying to write. Although Isobel was a very bright child and had lots of friends, she started not wanting to go to school. Her parents were concerned that their daughter seemed so unhappy in school, but they didn't understand what the problem was. It was a neighbor who suggested that Isobel be referred for an assessment.

Why didn't Isobel's elementary school recommend that she be tested? The unfortunate answer: schools don't typically recommend testing first-graders because they are in denial. Yes, schools can also be in denial about the needs of atypical children. Despite extensive research on the importance of early intervention, it is quite common for schools and even pediatricians to take a "wait-and-see" approach that ends up having the effect of "wait to fail." Administrators and teachers are aware that there is normal variation in the learning time-line of different children, so students are not screened until they show a profound lag in academic mastery or pronounced difficulty in social-emotional behaviors. In some schools, this means it can take until third grade or later to discover that a child is lagging. It is not uncommon for me to test children who are already in middle school or even high school and have somehow scraped by, eluding the casual and benign eye of their teachers for many years. Many a parent has said to me, "I trusted them to tell me if something was wrong, and no one said anything." The bottom line is, don't wait for a teacher to confirm something you already suspect in your gut. Have it checked out.

Isobel's parents eventually brought her to me when she was seven, at the end of first grade. When I tested her and told her parents that she had a mild form of dyslexia, Samantha and Ian didn't read the report closely and didn't follow up with the recommended remedia-tion. Their response was that Isobel's condition was "not so bad," so they would simply continue with occasional tutoring by their neigh-bor, who was an elderly retired schoolteacher.

The notion that all they needed was a tutor was a form of denial in this case, because hiring an occasional tutor is not the appropriate treatment of dyslexia. Dyslexia can be a stubborn condition that re-quires intensive hours of specific remediation in order to rewire the child's brain to read. It is not a temporary problem, and it demands a great deal of energy and specialized instruction to work through. Ignoring my report, however, Samantha and Ian viewed their daugh-ter's situation as "no big deal." In their opinion, Isobel merely lagged a little behind in attaining reading skills. "Everyone learns at his own pace," Ian told me. "She'll catch up. She's a really bright little girl." In fact, Isobel was very intelligent, but dyslexia is not related to one's level of intelligence. It is a reading disability that occurs when the brain does not properly recognize and process certain symbols.

Apparently, Ian gave little weight to the fact that Isobel was following in his own unhappy footsteps. As he had disclosed in our follow-up meeting, Ian and his mother were both severely dyslexic, and the condition had greatly affected their lives. Isobel's grandmother had left high school midway through tenth grade with a deep loss of self-esteem. She worked at menial jobs and never was able to improve herself, as she put it. Isobel's father, Ian, chose to attend a vocational school and is a talented furniture designer, compensating for his learning challenges by finding a career that did not require extensive reading. However, his lack of self-esteem was equal to that of his mother.

I didn't see Isobel for another three years. When I revisited her and her parents, Isobel was ten. Research on reading disorders shows that by that age, if a child is two years behind grade level, it is much more difficult to catch up than it would have been at age seven. But the fact that I had informed Samantha and Ian that Isobel had "a mild form of dyslexia" allowed them to lull themselves into a sense of denial. They hung on to the word *mild* and essentially ignored the word *dyslexia*. Ian told himself, "Well, I have that and I'm doing okay, so she'll be okay too." Ultimately, Isobel's parents failed to heed both the messenger and the message.

Part of the numbness parents experience in the denial phase is that they don't hear what they don't want to hear. Samantha and Ian didn't hear the full diagnosis of their daughter's condition, nor did they hear that it should be aggressively handled.

When I saw Isobel at age ten, she was very anxious and showing obsessive-compulsive symptoms due to her anxiety. Her self-esteem was low, she was school-phobic, and she was pretty miserable. She was also quite upset with her parents, because at that point she felt let down. She had been complaining about school since first grade and was still suffering. Her parents had been in denial about her special needs, but Isobel was not. She knew she had a condition that needed attention. "Why won't they help me?" she asked me in one of our meetings.

After years of denial, Samantha and Ian finally acknowledged that their daughter had been right all along. A significant amount of emotional damage had already been done, but at last Isobel got the help she needed to reclaim her potential and her future.

When One Parent Is in Denial and the Other Is Not

When parents differ over how to respond to their child's disorder, I think of their union as a "mixed marriage." A child needs two parents who agree on how to confront his or her learning challenge, but with two different perspectives, conflict is unavoidable—and what's best for the child can be overlooked. The child suffers, and so does the parents' relationship.

Trevor was Paige and Ted's third child; the couple was now divorced. Paige was concerned about the fact that Trevor had not reached his developmental milestones as quickly as her older kids. His language was delayed, and he didn't seem the least bit interested in hearing what other people had to say. He seemed to tune out easily. If he was told to go get his backpack or asked to help set the table, Trevor would respond, "Huh?" or "Huh, what'd you say?" Although Paige was worried, Ted insisted that nothing was wrong. He was convinced that Trevor was just lazy and immature because he had big brothers who always did everything for him. When parents are divorced, it can be particularly hard to work through these differences in perception.

When Trevor was in third grade, he was diagnosed with an auditory processing disorder (APD). APD is not a hearing problem;

DEFINITION: AUDITORY PROCESSING DISORDER

Auditory processing disorder (APD) is an umbrella term that describes a variety of conditions that affect how a person processes auditory information, which can significantly affect their ability to process new information and learn. As a discrete diagnosis, the condition is not accepted by psychologists or psychiatrists and there are those who believe that it is part of other coexisting diagnoses.

---

rather, it is a neurological defect that affects how the brain processes spoken language. This makes it difficult for the child to process verbal instructions or even filter out background noise in the classroom. Upon hearing the diagnosis, Ted immediately dismissed it. He had never heard of auditory processing disorder, and he told Paige, "The only problem with Trevor is that he lacks motivation. I know he's capable of doing what's expected of him if he simply tries harder." In fact, Ted had unrealistic expectations of Trevor and refused to believe that he couldn't achieve at the same level as his other children.

Ted had little patience with Paige's efforts to help their son. She was spending hours every night helping Trevor with his homework. Because Trevor did not take in what was going on in class, Paige would have to review the lessons with him in the evening. Ted accused Paige of spoiling Trevor, contributing to his dependency, and creating a disability where he felt there wasn't any. Ted's feeling was: *Kids are supposed to do homework, and that homework is supposed to take thirty minutes, not two hours. My ex is causing trouble for me. What's the real story here? Is she angling for more child support?*

What was happening in this family? Ted was in denial, which is a common first reaction when a parent hears that his or her son has a learning difference. Paige understood that Trevor had a problem and was trying to help. Because the couple was divorced and also had opposite reactions to their son's situation, the tension was high. Each distrusted the other, and Trevor was caught in the middle.

If you disagree with your parenting partner about whether your child has a condition of any kind, it's important to understand that your partner's denial is a common parental response. Some parents need time to accept and deal with the reality of their child's challenges, and the amount of time it takes to move beyond the denial phase can vary widely. Some parents are in denial for ten minutes, some for ten days, others for ten years. Obviously you don't want to wait years for your child to receive the treatment he or she needs. So what can you do to assure that your partner becomes a fully on-board parent of an atypical child—someone who acknowledges the validity of the diagnosis and supports the recommended treatment protocol?

The two things that are most important in breaking through denial are education and validation from others whom you trust, be it a family member or a professional. Education means learning about your child's particular condition, learning the basics of child development, and perhaps finding out more about your family's history of learning or behavioral differences. Educating yourself is essential, as is allowing yourself the time to learn and absorb the relevant information.

Giving yourself enough time to confront your own issues and painful emotions is also crucial. As we mentioned in Chapter 1, when you are given the news that your child has a disorder, all sorts of feelings may arise, from shame and embarrassment to sadness, frustration, anxiety, fear, and more. If you and your partner can allow yourselves to delve into your own personal histories and explore your feelings, it will pave the way toward accepting the reality of your child's diagnosis. Denial will no longer be an obstacle to getting help for your child.

A Gut Feeling: The Opposite of Denial

In most families, one parent usually suspects that a child has a learn-ing or behavioral difference before the other parent notices. This par-ent may not know where to turn for advice, particularly if his or her partner, relatives, pediatrician, and friends are not supportive. But a parent's gut feeling is almost always accurate, and it represents the opposite of denial.

I'll often get a call from a mom who will say something like, "My pediatrician thinks there's nothing wrong, the school thinks there's nothing wrong, but I think there's something wrong with my child, and I just want to check it out." I have learned over my twenty-five years of diagnosing children with neurodevelopmental issues that these moms (or dads) are very often correct in their hunches. So I tell my clients, "Trust your mommy (or daddy) gut. Don't let anyone tell you there's nothing wrong with your kid if you suspect that there might be."

I cannot tell you how many parents have sat in my office and sobbed when I validated everything about which they were worried. My professional assessment is a relief to them, because people had accused these moms and dads of being helicopter parents, overanx-ious parents, or obsessive parents. When family members are in de-nial about something that you feel in your gut is the truth—or which a professional has already verified—it's like having players on your team who don't share the same game plan. It can be extremely frus-trating for the parent who believes that something is wrong, has had her notion validated by a professional, and still must confront denial on the part of her partner or other relatives.

I've had parents bring doubting grandparents, aunts, and uncles into my office and say to me: "Explain it to them. Tell them what you told me. I really want everyone to know about our daughter's diagno-sis." I commend the moms and dads who bring in denying relatives, because then they, the un-denying parents, do not have to feel like they are alone in the field trying to catch the ball while everyone else on the team is throwing it in the opposite direction.

In my experience, mothers are the ones most likely to have a gut feeling about their child. Unfortunately, even in our allegedly liberated era, it sometimes seems as if no one is lower on the totem pole than a mom who thinks there's something wrong with her kid. She is often given no respect. Pediatricians sigh loudly, school officials shut their doors, and teachers after conferences roll their eyes as if to say, "Another complaining mother!" I've been at such meetings, and I've witnessed the eye rolling. So I am aware that there is a lot of gender inequality going on and way too much labeling of women as overanxious, "get-a-life" parents. Children with learning or behavioral differences would be much better served if these educators and health care professionals had the attitude "Let's take this parent seriously and listen to her concerns, because no one is watching this child as carefully as she is, and no one has as much invested in this child."

The gut feeling that something might be wrong with your child is the opposite of denial, and denial is not just limited to parents. Pediatricians, teachers, school officials, grandparents, neighbors, friends—they all can feed into the denial system, making parents question their own accurate perceptions. When Jane and Martin, parents with a history of dyslexia, asked the school to assess their five-year-old son who was already showing signs of dyslexia, the school counselor asked them, "He's doing fine; why are you so insistent on finding something wrong with him?"

Denial Is Part of a Process

Do any of the stories in this chapter resonate with you? Have you or someone close to you been stuck in denial? Have you felt like a deer in the headlights, struck numb and unable to decide what to do, who

to believe, what action to take? Maybe you have moved on and accepted your child's learning or behavioral difference, but you encounter denial every day with your spouse, your own parent, or a
well-intentioned neighbor. Maybe just one comment, raised eyebrow,
or doubtful stare can send you back into the paralysis of denial and
doubt.

Being in denial is not necessarily a one-way door; it can be a re-
volving one. One moment you are resolved and accepting, the next
moment you are thrust back into denial. Finding the inner resolve
that allows you to unfreeze, calm your emotions, and begin to think
rationally—so that you can permanently break through the denial—
is a process. Before the brain's thinking/decision making neocortex,
the brain's "top floor," comes out of its flash-frozen state during the
denial phase, its limbic system (the brain's "lower floor") is awakened.
This is your emotional brain, and when it awakens, it does so with a
roar. It is at this point that anger surges forth. We will explore that
phase in the next chapter. But first, I invite you to engage in the following guided imagery meditation, and also to consider self-care as
you transition through denial.

A Guided Imagery Meditation on Denial

Find a comfortable place to sit or lie down, somewhere where you
will not be disturbed. You may want to put on some music that you
find relaxing and peaceful. Close your eyes and breathe slowly and
deeply. Pay attention to your breath. Noticing your breathing will
slow you down and calm you.

Now imagine that you are holding a valued treasure in your
clenched fist. You don't want to lose it, so you grasp it more tightly.
As you grasp the treasure more tightly, you sense that there is a risk
of breaking it. The more tightly you grasp it, the more likely it is go-

ing to break. Imagine that the treasure represents your child, and your tightening grip represents your denial ("There is nothing wrong with my child!").

Ask yourself: "If I loosen my grip, will I lose that treasure—or will my child benefit?"

Ask yourself: "Who or what stands between me and my ability to learn more about my child's differences? Is it fear of the unknown? Fear of disapproval of others? Fear that my child might be different?"

De-catastrophize: "What's the worst that could happen?" This question is often used to de-catastrophize an upsetting situation. Once you visualize the worst, it will help you to see things in perspective and may spur you to take action.

Perspective: Take another perspective. Pretend that a friend of yours is in the same situation, and imagine what advice you would give him or her. Notice how much more compassionate you feel toward your imagined friend that you do toward yourself. Pay attention to the reasonable feelings and thoughts you are sharing with your imagined friend.

Accept your feelings: Allow yourself to feel whatever unpleasant feelings you are having. Try to detach and view those feelings from a distance. It's okay for those feelings to be with you—acceptance doesn't happen overnight. Allow yourself to feel compassion toward yourself as you move through this new set of doorways. It will not always feel this way. Even if it isn't feeling good now, it will feel better eventually.

Smile: Promise yourself to try to stay positive. Cultivating a happy attitude can help you remember the good times and let go of things that you cannot control. Remember, you did not become a parent to ensure that everyone and everything be perfect. Being cheerful on the outside (even if things on the inside aren't so great) can actually create more happiness for you and those around you.

Self-Care as You Transition through Denial

We have discussed how the shock of discovering that your child may have a learning or behavioral difference is often experienced as a kind of trauma. One of the principles of trauma therapy is that self-care can enable your brain to reregulate so that you can recover your sense of emotional balance.

What might that self-care look like for you? For some, it is a relaxing massage, a calming bubble bath, a quiet dinner with your loved one, a long walk with your dog, singing at the top of your lungs, or a bike ride in the woods. For others, it is being with a group of people who nourish your needs and understand you. And for others, it may be a good game of bowling. It is up to you to look for personal resources that you can return to whenever you need to nourish yourself and find "the old you"—the person you were before your nerves were frayed. Later in this book you will be introduced to the Self-Care Menu, which will help you discover the types of self-care that are most beneficial to you. For now, make a list of five calming or refreshing activities that you would enjoy, and promise yourself that you'll do one or more of those things at least once or twice a week.

Another form of self-care is to spend some reflective time alone with your child. Not to learn, not to train, not to have expectations, but just to be with him or her. Read a story, do an art project. Be mindful of the feelings that you have for each other. For many parents, having quiet time with their child (even if the quiet only lasts for a few moments) can help bolster their inner resources and calm their nerves. You may find yourself thinking, *See? My child is still my child.* Just because your son or daughter may have a diagnosis, this is still the child you know and love. Take the extra time to get to know your child on a deeper level.

Education is an essential element of your personal development as a parent. Where can you get more information about what the professionals are trying to tell you? What can you read? It's your responsibility to find out as much as you can about your child's diagnosis before you begin to put together an action plan. Even to deny a diagnosis requires an education.

Beware of sources you find on the Internet; there is simply too much conflicting material on it. Ask your pediatrician, your child's teacher or principal, your neuropsychologist, or your therapist if they know of any books that could enlighten you. Research. Don't jump to conclusions. Remember that the professionals who work with your child went to school for many years to learn about different disabilities, and most of them have your child's best interests at heart. As you read the books, highlight anything you do not understand and investigate further. By educating yourself, you will become a partner in this crusade, rather than a denier.

In Chapter 4, "Bargaining and Seeking Solutions," you will learn about people who can help you research your child's conditions and the various treatment options. There are groups you can form or join to defray costs, and there are even crowd-sourcing websites where you can turn for very cost-effective research. You don't have to do this alone. But for now, simply allow yourself to unclench your fist and be open to the possibilities. The opposite of denial is being curious and open, aware and loving. Try to keep that in mind as you proceed through this journey.

CHAPTER THREE

Anger and Blame

You know who I feel bad for? Me! My wife has no time for me, but our grandson has everything he needs: his grandma at his service 24/7, all the specialists that are costing me a fortune, and all that pressure to pay those bills. I'm so frustrated I could punch something. Or someone.

—Bill, grandfather of a five-year-old boy with autism

. . .

Bill and his wife, Leslie, had been Ryan's guardians since the boy was a year old. That's when their daughter, Ryan's mom, took off to live with her boyfriend in another state. Frustrated and upset by his grandson's erratic behavior, Bill often erupted in anger—at the professionals who tried to help Ryan, at his wife, and at Ryan. His explosive reactions were alienating to those who tried to help as well as those he loved most.

Why do so many parents become angry? Intellectually, everyone knows that anger is the most destructive emotion, and that it is nearly always counterproductive. At worst, anger has the potential to destroy the bonds that connect family members to one another. Yet anger is an enormous problem among many families raising atypical children. In Ryan's grandfather's case, underneath his anger were the anxiety and frustration he felt about Ryan's condition: *Why can't I fix this? Will my grandson ever be normal? Is it my fault? What am I supposed to do to make things better? I'm getting really tired of this.* These feelings are entirely understandable and predictable.

In the last chapter, we looked at denial as the initial response to the traumatic news that something is "wrong" with your child. Becoming numb and going on autopilot allows your mind to turn off the disturbing information about your child's condition. This enables you to function superficially and suppress your emotional responses until your brain recovers from the shock. As you slowly process the new facts, denial fades, and your brain is ready to move forward. But its attempts to surge into action probably will not result in a logical "let's solve this" plan of attack, not right away. Instead, your response may be akin to the roar from a momma bear whose cub is threatened—like a primitive howl of rage.

Paul Gilbert, author of *The Compassionate Mind*, notes that anger comes from three specific types of fear: fear of being hurt or destroyed, fear of having no control over your life goals, and fear of being marginalized, ignored, excluded, or isolated.[1] Parents of atypical children are often awash in fear. The fear you feel about your child can even be experienced as physical pain: a literal ache in your heart, a throbbing headache that won't go away, or any number of other symptoms. In addition to being afraid for your child, you might fear that you won't be able to help, that your "abnormal" kid makes you look like a failure, that your relationship with your partner will wither under the strain, that life as you know it is going to change forever. Those fears, as well as others, engulf many parents as the numbing effect of denial wanes. The fear often boils to the surface in angry outbursts at anyone or everyone, sometimes including the child.

How Your Anger Affects Your Child's World

Anger has predictable patterns. As a distinct phase of coming to grips with your child's diagnosis, anger can be temporary, come in

waves, or become chronic. Much depends on your natural temperament combined with your perception of the current situation. When
faced with the news that a child has a disorder, even parents who are
normally mellow and optimistic can feel surges of anxiety that erupt
into angry outbursts. People who are not naturally easygoing but
have a history of aggression and belligerence are, not surprisingly,
more apt to lash out and try to defend their turf at the slightest hint
of threat. Parents are people too, people with backgrounds, personality types, and individual reactions to life situations. Some of them
become hostile or even abusive when faced with circumstances that
are unexpected, overwhelming, and threatening to their family.

It's a fact of life that parenthood comes with anxieties and surprise detours. One needn't have an atypical child to experience anger
and its fallout. All parents should be aware of the crushing and un-
intended consequences their anger can have on their children. But
the anger I am describing here is a specific one that emanates from
the realization that your family is now on a path that differs from
what you expected. This upset can translate into flashes of anger,
long-term bitterness, or sarcastic or hostile jokes that end up distanc-
ing you from others. Or internal stress that explodes into rage when
it becomes too much to hold internally.

Learning about the anger response is critical. How you handle
your anger influences the way you will be received (and helped) by
professionals, how you will develop a community of supporters to
help you with your child, whether your family thrives or breaks apart,
and how your child's self-esteem develops.

Anger has a way of spreading outward, like the ripples from a
pebble thrown into a pond. Our energy is contagious. Positive energy
breeds positive relationships. Be around happy people and you will
be more cheerful. Be around angry or hostile people and you will find
yourself being drawn into a negative mindset. This phenomenon has
great implications for your family and affects the entire team you
want to build in order to help your child. Positive, plucky parents who

bring treats to staff meetings to thank their child's team or otherwise express gratitude help create positive energy that can enhance the outcome of their child's therapy. Parents who show up to these meetings hostile or withdrawn, or who make negative or belligerent comments, are seen as difficult and do not promote the culture of cooperation that your child needs.

Now, I understand why parents may be defensive or confrontational in these meetings. Many of the meetings are dreadful. Parents can feel outnumbered—often a single parent can be surrounded by a team of ten or more professionals, each speaking dispassionately about your child. They may be using numbers and confusing acronyms (OHI? IEP? SLP?) as they make critical decisions about your precious son or daughter. If you are a full-time working parent, you have had to ask for time off in the middle of your working day for a meeting that could take several hours, all for the school's convenience. You enter a room and feel that you are entering in the middle of a conversation with a predetermined course. About your child. It's normal and understandable to feel powerless, threatened, suspicious, and angry. But for your child's sake, you must not let these feelings sabotage your relationships with these professionals. Try to remember that having an atypical child means that you will be working within a team approach. These professionals are experts in whatever particular condition affects your child. Yet you are the ultimate expert on your child. Share. Be collaborative. Teamwork does work.

Our energy is contagious. Positive energy breeds positive relationships.

So, catch yourself at the door and look inside yourself for a moment. Many parents don't realize how angry they are feeling or how hostile they come across to other people. If they saw a video of themselves, they might be shocked. A good number of them would probably rationalize their behavior—they're under so much stress, and the situation is so unfair. They justify their anger and don't realize how much damage they're doing. But for every time you say "Not me" while reading this chapter, think again. Notice your tone. Notice your reactions. Notice how your body feels. My goal is to help you become more self-aware, so that you can take back control of your life. Being aware of your feelings and learning to manage them is fundamental to everything you want to achieve for yourself and your child.

It is a given that something about your atypical child is going to push your buttons. Children who process information differently, or talk or walk more slowly, or need extra assistance with self-care, or become rowdy at exactly the wrong times are more likely to spark anger in their parents. It's important to realize that your anger (or your spouse's) needs tending. Anger seeks an outlet, as we'll discuss throughout this chapter. In addition to alienating health care professionals, unchecked anger has a tremendously negative impact on family life. The rates of divorce and child abuse are high in families with atypical children. Even if the parents stay together and do not abuse their child, their anger can be corrosive. While all children dislike it when their parents yell at them or fight with each other, atypical children are less able than the average child to tolerate the shouting and the negative atmosphere. One common result is that the child's self-esteem—nearly always an issue anyway—will plunge even lower.

If you are a professional who works with special-needs children, I strongly advise you to look again at the parents you are dealing with, especially the most difficult ones—the defensive, hostile, threatening parents. In order to work effectively with them, you need to realize that underneath their anger is fear, deep disappointment, and anxiety about losing control. Learning about the anger phase can give you valuable insights and help you forge an alliance with these parents in support of their child. Angry parents are not necessarily uncooperative parents. Find out what is going on. Chances are, they are feeling marginalized or anxious about having a child with a diagnosis, or they just finished arguing with their spouse before coming in to your office. Don't be afraid to ask parents about how they are doing. Tending to the parents is an important part of helping the child.

The Neuropsychology of Anger: Inside the Brain of the Momma (or Poppa) Bear

We humans are hardwired to react to our feelings. All feelings generate hormonal responses that then demand some type of discharge of energy. When you receive wonderful news that makes you feel happy—for instance, hearing that you got a raise—you might burst into song or do a victory dance down the hall. It's a happy adrenaline surge that expresses itself through body communication. So too with anger.

Anger is a powerful emotion, one of the seven basic emotional states that are hardwired not only into humans but also into most mammals.[2] Anger generates an aggressive response. In the body, anger releases a surge of cortisol, the stress hormone that can elevate blood pressure and create tension. Emotionally, anger triggers irritability, hostility, aggressiveness, nervousness. Chronic anger can lead to anxiety or depression, and chronic anxiety can lead to angry outbursts.

When you are angry, you will have an immediate physical reaction. You may experience:

- A rush of adrenaline
- Rapid pulse
- Uneven, pounding heart
- Shortness of breath, panting
- Sweating
- Sudden urge to shout or break something
- Stomachache

- Headache
- Urge to act, but difficulty thinking

Anger as an emotion isn't always a bad thing. In evolutionary terms, when humans and animals struggled for survival, anger served an important function: It stimulated action and prompted them to fight off threats against themselves or their offspring. In response to feelings of perceived danger or pain, your brain shoots action signals from the amygdala to the muscles and organs of your body. (The amygdala is a small structure found in the limbic system and associated with emotions and aggression, particularly anger.) This surge of neurochemicals creates an immediate and single-minded focus: *Crush the perceived threat.*

Anger is primitive and often impulsive. Although the brain is wired to experience anger, an unprocessed anger response is seldom a wise choice. At its most basic level, anger represents a universal life force. It is the organism's vigorous attempt at self-preservation. Evolutionarily speaking, anger was very useful. For our modern times—not so much.

When you are hit with distressing news (for instance, your child's diagnosis, or seeing your child act strangely at a birthday party and realizing that something is really wrong), you may initially freeze like the proverbial deer in the headlights. Your brain is processing potentially threatening information and attempting to fit it into the mental landscape that currently exists—"reality" as you have known it until that point. "Reality" is a set of perceived notions that have created a specific set of neurological pathways in your memory patterns. The unexpected and threatening news disrupts those pathways—your numbness is the brain groping to find some way to compute the new information. When the numbness fades, your mind must shift gears and try to set fresh pathways that can integrate the news. It is not always a graceful or predictable process.

Anger that follows denial often is a result of grasping that this news *is* in fact a potential threat to you and your child. "What?" you may sputter, "Why is my kid acting so odd?" and you may look for a target on which to vent your rage. "Did you see if there's a bully here who upset my kid? No wonder he's all huddled up in a corner, scared to move! Where's that bully's dad? I'm going to go have a word with him!" The neocortex (the thinking brain) provides rational control over our emotions, filtering out our most primitive responses, but in the moment of rage, it loses its ability to reason. As Daniel Goleman puts it, the amygdala has hijacked the brain.[3] He notes, "Emotions make us pay attention right now—this is urgent—and give us an immediate action plan without having to think twice. The emotional component evolved very early: Do I eat it, or does it eat me?"[4]

This is true not only when you first hear threatening news but also when you continue to gather confirming information about the threatening news. Bill, who reacted so negatively to his grandson's behavior in the vignette at the beginning of this chapter, did not always explode like that. Although he was aggressive by nature, he had learned over the years to control it. Experience in the world had trained his neocortex to mediate his angry feelings through discussing the problem or by planning for situations that would be emotionally challenging. But times of high stress—say, after a long day at work, with bills waiting on his desk at home and Ryan throwing his nightly tantrum—temporarily shorted those circuits of reason and logic. Bill's amygdala hijacked his reasoning brain and he would frequently become a storm of rage, frightening his wife and terrifying Ryan.

While all strong emotions demand a discharge of energy, anger requires a target—usually a human target. We don't need another person to be happy or sad with; we can just feel those emotions. We can be afraid of a burglar or of an avalanche. But while we can hate our lemon of a car, we can't really be angry at it. We are angry with the person who sold us the car. Likewise with anger about our child's condition. While our rage may spread to include society at large, fate, or modern medicine, our anger usually focuses on more specific targets. We can't be angry at an inanimate concept such as ADHD or autism. We have to be angry at someone. *Who will we blame?*

The Nearest Target: Our Partner

A parent's anger may be aimed at a variety of people: teachers, pediatricians, school officials, friends, family members. Sometimes parents even blame the child with the disorder. But the person most often in the line of fire is the parent who is the primary caretaker—this usually is the mother. Throughout our most recent social history, mothers have been blamed for causing untold harm to children. Most of these theories were eventually proven false. But psychology is littered with references to refrigerator mothers, overprotective mothers, neurotic mothers, dysfunctional mothers, premenstrual and hormonal mothers. In the case of families where a child has a disorder, Mother is still often seen as the "perpetrator" of this miserable hardship, especially if she tends to be emotional. Of course, psychology textbooks are full of blame for fathers as well. Distant fathers, uninvolved fathers, workaholic dads, alcoholic dads, aggressive dads, too-macho-to-change-diapers dads. When parents blame each other, they often engage in impassioned battles, accusing, defending, and exacerbating an already tense situation, often bringing in outmoded stereotypes to bolster their reasoning.

No one enters into parenthood with another person intending to blame that person for a child's problems. But too often, the stress of having to cope with the tedium and fears of managing a difficult situation, dealing with one too many public tantrums or too many doctor visits, can lead parents to attack the only other adult who is next to them in the trenches. An angry father or mother may insist that the child's disorder is because of the other parent's bad genes or shoddy parenting. "You babied him, you ignored him, you pressured him." Or "Your family has a history of mental illness—that's why our kid is so messed up."

One of the saddest aspects of parents blaming each other is when Mom agrees with the blamer and blames herself for their child's difficulties. (The opposite—Dad blaming himself—occurs less often, but it does happen.) I can't count the number of mothers who have told me, "I must be a terrible mom," or "I wish I knew what I was doing wrong!" or "I think about what I ate during pregnancy," or "I was working full-time—is it my fault for not being there to properly stimulate him?" Their statements often begin with "I know it's silly but I can't help wondering . . ." Self-blame is not only tragic and debilitating, but it is also nearly always nonproductive. (We will delve more deeply into the psychology of self-blame in Chapter 5, "The Depression Trap.")

Many divorces occur as a result of angry (and often mistaken) accusations that erupt between parents. This is not surprising, given the pressures that may become too much for some couples to handle. Fortunately, understanding the role of anger and how it can be controlled can make a big difference in parents' behavior.

Parents need to accept and acknowledge to each other that their child's condition—whether a learning disability, autism, OCD, Tourette's, ADHD, epilepsy or a genetic disease—is not directly due to any one thing. While parenting techniques can and do affect a child's development, in all likelihood, this child's diagnosis is not because of Mom's disorganized housekeeping or Dad's relative disinterest in daily activities. Good parenting is a critically important factor in raising a healthy and successful child, but the truth is that some children do not start out as soundly wired as others. Decades of research into neurodevelopmental disorders shows that even the most well-balanced parents can have children who are atypical. It happens to all types of families. Additionally, rates of many conditions are on the rise. An increasing number of children are developing atypically, learning differently, and facing more challenges in integrating into the typical school/social network. This is an equal opportunity phenomenon, with increasing levels of diagnoses affecting all strata of society.

Factors That May Affect a Child's Development

What exactly are we talking about when we say that a child has a neurodevelopmental disorder? Human brains are wired to develop in a systematic and largely predictable way in order to reach anticipated benchmarks in expected time frames. But many children do not develop in expected ways. They may be delayed in some manner but not in others. Brain research and research by leading neuroscientists from around the world tell the story: There are clear differences between the brains of people with developmental differences and those without those conditions. Let's take a look at some of the factors that, according to the latest research, can contribute to atypical brain development:

Heredity. Learning disabilities or other disorders often run in the family. It is not uncommon to find that people with learning disabilities have parents or other relatives with similar difficulties. Neurobiological and genetic research has suggested genetic attributes and a "neural signature" for dyslexia (the most prevalent and well-understood subtype of learning disability). Rather than using this to blame the parent with the genetic pattern, find out how this parent or relative handled the disability. What are the keys to success? A parent with dyslexia or ADHD can be an excellent source of support for a child with the same condition. Or maybe now is the time for this parent to get help for him- or herself, further serving as a role model for the child.

Problems during pregnancy, birth, and in the neonatal period.
It happens. Every pregnancy is different. Many different types of
disorders may be caused by lack of oxygen at birth, neonatal disease, myriad illnesses, or injury before or during birth. These
conditions may also be caused by low birth weight, drug and alcohol use during pregnancy, and premature or prolonged labor.
Incidents after birth could include head injuries (active babies do
roll!), nutritional deprivation, and exposure to toxic substances
(such as lead). Many of the families I see wonder if their child's
condition is due to an early issue. The truth is, in most cases the
answer is not clear and no one can point to a single event. As an
example, I have worked with a number of children who had pre-
natal polysubstance exposure or fetal alcohol symptoms. Some
seemed impacted and others were just fine, for no discernable
reason.

Physical illness. A child with a physical illness might exhibit
patterns of learning or behavioral differences that are part of the
illness, as is the case with neurofibromatosis (a genetic disorder
of the nervous system that affects how nerves form and grow).
This disease, among many others, creates a strong likelihood of
learning disabilities. Other children with early birth defects or
born prematurely may thrive physically but have problems that
show up later, such as learning disabilities, ADHD, or other disorders. Again, the severity and level of impact varies from child
to child, with no apparent reason.

Genetics interacting with environment. In the case of autism
spectrum disorders (ASD), scientists are not sure of the cause,
but it is likely that both genetics and environment play a role.
Researchers have studied the brains of people with ASD and
found irregularities in several of the brain's regions; in addition,
researchers have identified various genes associated with au-

tism. Still other studies focused on the levels of serotonin and other neurotransmitters in the brains of people with ASD, and discovered that they vary from the norm. The disruption may take place early in fetal development, and it could also be caused by some type of environmental influence on gene function. All of these theories are far from conclusive. What *is* conclusive is that neither parenting styles nor vaccines cause autism.

Unknown. Frustratingly, there are many conditions for which the cause is simply not known. Examples would include children who are exceptionally anxious, or obsessive and rigid, or who have vague neurological syndromes for which there is not a general diagnosis. In fact, there is frequently no apparent cause for many quirky issues, learning disabilities, ADHD, autism, intellectual disabilities, and neurological or chromosomal disorders.

Regardless of why a child has a particular condition, this point bears repeating: The architecture of the brain of a child who learns or behaves atypically is clearly different from the norm. In the overwhelming majority of cases, these brain differences are not due to bad parenting or indifferent schools or even poor living conditions. Certainly, a terrible home environment is not advised for growing children; families with tension, constant yelling, or chronic stress can deeply impact a child. Schools without sufficient identification or remediation resources can surely be faulted for lack of early identification and support of many children. Poverty and stressful living situations hinder parents from getting care for their children; it has also been shown that severe levels of stress do indeed affect brain function. However, there are also resilient children who emerge from stressful childhoods intact. Researchers are trying to figure out why some children weather their difficult childhoods and go on to become successful, against all odds.

The complex truth is, there are genetic and biological factors that predispose some children to learn or behave atypically. In my practice, I always ask parents about their child's genetic history, and in many instances there are family members with similar markers. I often tell parents, "We all have genes, and no one can be held culpable for their genetic makeup." But as much as I say this, there are those who continue to blame their spouse or their own parents for their child's atypicality. Anger needs a target, and a spouse or grandparent is often the one with the convenient bull's-eye on his or her back. We are all descended from a variety of ancestors with "differences." No one has a perfect gene pool.

People are at their angriest when they feel helpless or hopeless. Those who are anxious, emotionally reactive, or who grew up in angry households are most at risk. At the end of this chapter, there will be tools to help you work with yourself and move toward a more serene state of mind. These techniques will also help you be more at peace with your child's situation, and both of you will benefit.

> *When angry, count to ten before you speak. If very angry, count to one hundred.*
>
> —Thomas Jefferson

Shifting the Blame from Teachers and the School

I've heard many parents heatedly assert that their child's learning or behavior difficulties are due to poor teaching, a teacher who was too strict or too lenient, one who "refused to discipline my kid," or "didn't teach phonics and reading the way we were taught," or "traumatized her and made her withdraw." In the grip of their anger, parents cling to the belief that a teacher can turn an otherwise "normal" child into one with a learning disability or atypical personality—which is rarely the case, even if the teacher is ineffective or insensitive.

Schools can be blamed for a lot of things, but most teachers don't deserve the wrath they receive from irate parents when children show signs of learning differences, asocial behaviors, or hyperactivity, or if they have special needs in the classroom. It is estimated that as many as 10 to 20 percent of school-age children in the United States will display some type of learning problem or delay, and the percentage is higher if you include children who will exhibit a behavior problem.[5] This clearly can't all be linked to bad teachers or indifferent school personnel.

Sometimes a parent's anger is directed not at the teacher but at school officials who "should have switched our son into a different class," or "never told us our daughter was being teased on the playground," or "have no reason to keep our child out of regular classes," or "provide a terrible curriculum." School officials may be guilty of these failures, but school policies do not *cause* a child to develop atypically. However, their indifference or failure to act can certainly be infuriating. I am not trying to excuse incompetent or indifferent principals or teachers. But a parent's natural default mode is to become angry, which does little to improve a particular situation.

It's true that many schools are slow to identify learning differences and some behavioral differences in children. Change is coming, but not fast enough. Schools (and pediatricians) are beginning to understand that early identification is extremely important for the atypical child's future. There are critical windows of learning for mastery of certain skills. Unfortunately, many school districts still employ a "wait-to-fail" model of intervention; that is, children must demonstrate a substantial gap in skills before they "qualify" for remedial services. This is tragic in so many ways. Children can be identified and remediated at much younger ages than is currently in common practice. Autism often can be identified in preschool, dyslexia by age six, and developmental disorders no later than first grade. The fact that I regularly diagnose common disorders for the first time in teenagers and people in their twenties indicates that many children are slipping through the cracks of the system.

Often, the anger parents feel toward the school system or gatekeepers to service is legitimate. It is not wrong to feel angry, but demonstrating your anger is an ineffective and destructive response to the problems. Being "that parent" in the school meeting or carpool drop-off line isn't going to win you any favors, nor is it likely to win you allies among other parents.

Ah, but sometimes anger feels so good! Especially when you're right. Righteous anger has amphetamine and analgesic effects, meaning that it temporarily makes you feel strong, imbues you with confidence and power, and numbs your pain. Righteous anger is difficult to negotiate because although you *are* right, it will not help with your dilemma.

It's exhausting and frustrating to navigate the bureaucracy and learn how to work the system effectively. In many cases, even after you have done all that, you realize that the support that's available will not really serve your child. Take a high-functioning autistic (HFA) child who is placed in a special day class with children who are severely autistic and OHI (other health impaired). It's unlikely that this will be a good match, your gut tells you, because your child needs positive role models. Are you right? Of course you are! But this day class is what is available. So you need to calm your anger and work out another strategy, such as volunteering in the classroom, lobbying for better services, or hiring an advocate (or in some cases an attorney) who can assist you. When your child is atypical, there might not be a perfect fit of custom-made services. That is the frustrating reality. But you can work with your environment to build that support system. It will take a carefully constructed army with you as the general, not your anger, to help your child.

Productive Anger: Getting the Truth from Reluctant Teachers

Maggie and Kevin were the parents of an eight-year-old son, Eric. They came in to see me because Eric was in the third grade and still not reading. After testing him, I identified why Eric, a delightful child with a winning sense of humor, was very delayed in his reading and writing skills. Eric had dyslexia. Yet according to Maggie and Kevin, Eric's school had not disclosed any pertinent information about how their son was performing academically. There were no grades or report cards sent home, because Eric's progressive private school did not believe in them. His teachers (there were several) and the school administrators really liked Eric and his family and, it seemed, wanted to downplay the boy's struggle with academics. And Maggie and Kevin went along with this for a few years, ignoring their instincts that something was amiss, lulled into a group denial. Then, at the end of third grade, the school informed them that they were a bit concerned about Eric's progress and suggested testing to see if he should repeat third grade.

In this case, the parents' anger stemmed from the fact that they were feeling marginalized from the process of decision making about their child. "We were so frustrated," Kevin told me. "Here he was going to this supposedly terrific school with a staff of highly proficient teachers—and he couldn't read! And no one seemed to notice or care. One teacher I spoke with told me, 'Oh, don't rush him. They all eventually learn at their own pace.' And then all of a sudden they tell us about their concerns? That just wasn't cutting it in my book."

I asked Kevin and Maggie to identify the emotional triggers that this situation created for them. Over a few sessions, we talked about their anger at feeling left out, not being consulted early on, and not being included as real partners in their child's learning, which led to feelings of anger at the teachers and administrators. In that time they were able to digest what had occurred and calm down enough to use their angry energy to create a plan. Kevin and Maggie were scheduled for a team meeting. This meeting was going to include three teachers, an assistant teacher, principal, assistant principal, learning specialist, nurse, and PE teacher. That's nine professionals altogether; it seemed as if Kevin and Maggie were going to be outnumbered. I asked them to process in advance their feelings about being at such an intimidating meeting. What were their goals? What feelings was this triggering for them? How was this new information going to help them?

The meeting didn't go exactly to script but did get the desired results. After ninety minutes of listening to each teacher report on how Eric was doing in each subject, Kevin finally bluntly asked, "Will he be able to progress to fourth grade in the fall?"

The teachers admitted that Eric's skills were not on par with the other kids in his classroom and they were not sure if he could succeed in the fourth grade. At that point, Kevin got really angry and shouted sarcastically. "Well, thank you for finally letting us know! If you had told us this two years ago, we could have gotten help for Eric then!"

Kevin was understandably angry, but because he had anticipated and made a plan in advance, that energy led him and Maggie to make the very appropriate decision to put Eric in a special-needs school. I applaud them for transforming their anger into action. Their story is an excellent example of how healthy parental anger can get something positive accomplished. Handling anger appropriately actually helped propel them to do what was best for their little boy.

Shifting the Blame from the Doctors

Along with blaming the teacher and school system for not paying close enough attention to their child, parents may also focus their frustration and anger on their pediatrician or other doctors involved in the child's care. We count on doctors to have all the answers and give us the right advice about our child's condition. The pediatrician usually sees a child multiple times a year; we may even have brought certain symptoms to the doctor's attention, only to be told, "You worry too much—let's wait and see how things look in six months." Many parents have bitterly complained to me, "If only our pediatrician had noticed this earlier!" But while an early diagnosis is definitely an advantage in terms of intervention, it isn't helpful to look backward. Nevertheless, parents are understandably alarmed and angry when they think about the steps they could have been taking.

Most pediatricians I know are wonderful doctors who care deeply about their patients. However, even the best pediatrician is usually at a loss when a parent says, "Something is wrong with my child and I'm not sure what it is." Doctors have limited time to spend with each child in a standard office visit, and they primarily focus on physical health and development. Many are neither trained in nor attuned to subtle learning, attention, or personality issues. Plenty of typically developing children look abnormal in the doctor's office, because most kids are terrified of shots and examinations. So it's a tough call on the part of the pediatrician.

Pediatricians spend much of their time soothing nervous new parents. They do a wonderful job of helping parents get over anxieties concerning typical child-rearing challenges. It's not surprising, given this focus, that they sometimes miss signs of developmental difficulties that they perhaps should have seen. Despite that, the doctor is not to blame for your child's condition. If you are reading this and feel like your doctor is not fully on board with your concerns, call the doctor's office and ask for an extended appointment. Most doctors will be happy to spend time to hear you out if they have the time scheduled.

Many parents come to see me with only a vague suspicion that something is amiss, often despite teachers and pediatricians who reassure them that they need to take a "wait-and-see" approach. In the majority of cases, these brave parents are correct in their hunches, since parents know their children best. If you're reading this and your gut is telling you something may be wrong, first talk to your doctor and then get your child tested by a professional such as a neuropsychologist, who will take the time to listen to you, work with your child, and do a careful analysis of how your child functions. Move off the blame train and take action.

Shifting the Blame from the Grandparents, Nanny, or Other Family Members

In this era of single parents and nontraditional families, grandparents and other relatives are often a child's part-time caretakers. Blaming them for a child's learning difficulties or behavioral issues thus makes sense in the eyes of an upset parent. A distressed parent may toss out such accusations as "Why didn't they see this was happening?" or "They had kids already, they had experience in this area, why didn't they notice?"

A child may have relationships with a lot of family members, some of whom keep their personal feelings private in an effort to not offend or worry the parents. The nanny may not want to lose her job. Your expectation that other people should be your detectives is understandable but misguided; since you are the primary caretaker, it isn't likely that they will take the initiative and suggest that something is amiss. Or . . . maybe they did. Maybe someone told you about unusual behavior, or at least hinted at it, but your denial defenses were too strong and you simply didn't hear the message. Memory is idiosyncratic and selective—it can suppress information that is too inconvenient or uncomfortable. That's why eyewitness testimony is notoriously unreliable. Memory is always filtered through the emotional brain system, which decides what is salient enough to retain. In your child's case, maybe you did not notice, until now.

Shifting the Blame from Life, Vaccines, the Environment, Other People

Angry that such an awful fate has befallen their family, parents may focus their fury on a larger target. They may blame:

- The universe ("Life just isn't fair!")
- The current culture ("If we lived in another time or society, there would be more tolerance for kids who are a little different.")
- Vaccines ("I *know* they caused my son's autism!")
- The environment ("It's the toxins in our food and pollutants that have done this to my child.")
- Their community ("Why does everyone look so smug and cheerful? I hate all those women in the mommy-and-me classes. Their kids don't have these problems! We need to find a less uptight neighborhood—or country!")

Blaming the culture for your family's distress is entirely understandable. Social media in particular has an unhealthy emphasis on perfection: Our children are expected to be physically gorgeous, socially gregarious, athletically gifted, attain straight A's, and oh, yes, excel in at least one or two unusual passions such as playing the bassoon or creating a charitable website for orphans in Haiti. Little girls in grammar school worry that they're too fat. The culture's expectation of perfection pressures our children and also serves to emphasize our "failure" as parents to produce this perfect progeny. Many—*way* too many—parent gatherings descend into bragging sessions about the children's accomplishments, resulting in parents of atypical children avoiding these events entirely. Friendships are even severed due to parents' angry feelings (and depression, which we will talk about in a later chapter).

The problem with blaming our culture or other outside forces is that ultimately it is a waste of energy—and if there's one thing you're going to need as you raise your child, it is energy. My heart goes out to the many parents of autistic children who poured time, money, and effort into anti-vaccine activism, but there is no evidence that vaccines cause autism, and I do hope that parents who want to be activists can shift their attention and energy to a cause that will directly help their child or other children. Maybe activism is a good path for you; just try to be honest with yourself about why you are choosing that path, and why you have zeroed in on a particular cause. Does it feel better to stay in righteous anger than to move to acceptance and deal with the day-to-day challenges of raising your child? Keep in mind that intense anger about your child's condition is a phase you can pass through, if you want to. It is, at least partly, a choice you make.

> **Intense anger about your child's condition is a phase you can pass through, if you want to.**

Shifting the Blame Away from Yourself

Many parents feel tremendously guilty about their child's condition. They turn their anger inward and blame themselves. "If only I had figured this out sooner! I'm such a bad parent! Why didn't I see this coming?" These well-meaning moms and dads feel that if they had been stricter, more demanding, more attentive, or more sensitive it would have altered their child's condition. Of course, any condition can be made worse by anger, hostility and blame, chaotic households, and general lack of attentive parenting. At the very least, angry parents can make it harder for an atypical child to work at the top of his or her ability. That's why it is always appropriate to reexamine your parenting skills and the atmosphere inside your home.

That said, the problems of *most* of the atypical children visiting my office (and the offices of hundreds of neuropsychologists like me) are not the result of bad parenting. Most of the parents I see are well-meaning and worried about their children. When I reassure them that their child's condition is probably not due to "bad parenting," relief washes over their faces. It's important to have this discussion with parents, because guilt and self-blame can lead to depression. We'll talk about this more in Chapter 5, "The Depression Trap," but for now, let's look at the self-blaming comments I have heard most often.

Don't Let This Become You: Guilt Trips You Should Not Lay On Yourself

- I worked full-time when he was a baby; I must have disrupted his attachment process.
- Pregnancy was a really stressful time.
- When I was pregnant, I must have inhaled paint fumes while preparing the nursery.
- What did I eat that was harmful during pregnancy?
- I did not prepare properly for having a baby.
- Our home isn't—(nice enough, neat enough, in a good enough neighborhood).
- I have migraines, so I can't be as attentive to my child as I would like.
- I'm a terrible organizer—his desk is a mess; he got that from me—I don't even know how to help him clean it up.
- After dinner, I am so busy with work that I can't keep on top of her homework.
- We both work full-time and come home stressed.
- The birth was so traumatic that I haven't recovered and overreact to every little thing she does.
- His grandparent was (severely ill, died) while he was a small child, and this must have affected his personality.
- My husband and I don't get along, we try not to fight in front of

our child but somehow she knows anyway, that's why she is so anxious.

- We are a gay couple and maybe that has affected our child's development.
- I try to make nutritious meals, but his diet is still not great. I'm sure it's all about his diet.
- What are we doing wrong?
- Our child is adopted. We should have been better prepared.
- Maybe we are too old to be good parents.
- I didn't notice my child's condition soon enough.

Do any of these sound familiar? Of course they do, because we all worry we're going to mess up our kids. But blaming yourself for what might have happened in the past does nothing to help your child right now. Instead, self-blame becomes habitual and chips away at your emotional resilience, bit by bit. In the event that you continue to blame yourself for your child's differences despite your best rational conversation with yourself, try to remember that you are doing the best you can. Part of becoming an emotionally sound parent is developing the capacity for self-forgiveness. If you can do that, it will help the anger inside of you dissolve.

Shifting the Blame Away from Your Child

The most painful way that anger gets expressed is when parents target the child. We need only look at the social services roster to see how kids are too often blamed for things not under their control. According to a recent study, children with disabilities are three to four times more likely than those without disabilities to become victims of violence.[6] That's one in four atypical children at risk of abuse.

Parents can become intensely angry at their atypical children. Often, a child reminds parents of themselves when they were that age, of struggles or issues that were unresolved or of painful memories. The intensity of anger that parents exhibit toward their children tends to reflect the amount of self-care—or lack of it—the parents allow themselves to have. Put another way, parents who are taking care of their own needs and are not overwhelmingly anxious about their family's well-being tend to have greater tolerance for their children's behavior. A mom who is stressed out and takes an afternoon off for a massage or a hike in the park, then meets her friend for coffee and is able to talk about her problems and say good-bye with a big hug—that mom will be calmer and more patient with her child and the rest of the family when she gets home. The same goes for fathers. Taking care of yourself should not be an occasional perk or a reward for an especially harrowing day, but a part of your routine. As we repeat so often in this book, your child's well-being depends on your own mental health, and at no time is this more true than when you are learning to manage your anger.

Unfortunately, I have personally seen the results of parents' unrestrained anger. There have been times where I have had to call Child Protective Services and advise them that a family needs to be investigated. It's not a call I relish, but in some cases it's necessary. Atypical children, caught in the behaviors or conditions that make them atypical, can be so upsetting that some parents lose control and mete out punishment that is harsh or abusive. Luckily, most do not. But one in four is a very alarming statistic.

Even when a parent or guardian's anger toward the child doesn't result in physical abuse, it can manifest as emotional abuse. Lashing out at a child with a learning difference or behavioral problems with words such as "Stop being so needy and just do your homework!" or "If you weren't so lazy, you wouldn't have this problem!" will only result in a more traumatized child. I realize that children who are atypical do not make it easy on their parents. The nightly challenge of having to cope with an atypical child can stretch you to the breaking point. Some children won't or can't do their homework or sit through a meal. In some households, the bedtime routine is a time-bending agony for all involved—the most stressful part of the day. The relentlessness of the situation, especially if you do not yet have a support system and a plan in place, can make you feel desperate, trapped, helpless, and furious.

Despite all that, it is crucial that you refrain from taking out your anger on your child. Understanding how your child processes information may inspire you to find better ways to communicate with him or her, even when you feel anger bubbling up.

Brain Development in Atypical Children Is Often Asymmetrical

When children have learning or developmental disorders, they process information differently. There are neurophysiological reasons for this. Simply put, when information flows into the brain of such a person, the brain's circuitry scrambles it and the information can be inaccurate or distorted. Neurological dysfunction results in various learning, communication, and behavioral problems. This is true for children who have autism, ADHD, learning disabilities, processing disorders, neurological disorders, or emotional issues, despite these all being very different conditions. Even unimpaired children will sometimes process information differently than adults, because their brains are not as fully responsive or developed as adult brains. The very important executive function skills necessary for planning, problem solving, and flexible reasoning are immature in young brains. On average, executive function is not fully developed until the mid-twenties and beyond.

So it's a fact: Your atypical child processes information differently from the way you expect. It can sometimes appear as if the wires in his or her brain are plugged into faulty circuits or that your child is intentionally ignoring, avoiding, or doing exactly the opposite of what you request. While it is true that even typical kids will often process information differently than adults expect, your atypical child processes information differently much more frequently. But your kid is not more lazy, avoidant, manipulative, or stubborn than typical kids. In fact, many children with disorders have to work extra hard to do the things that come easily to typical children. They face relentless discouraging burdens that their differences create for them. Sadly, they may not get a lot of high-fives for following a simple direction or remembering a basic task, despite the all the effort that it takes.

In addition to processing information differently, the brains of many atypical children develop in a pattern of "asymmetry"—that is, in unpredictable growth spurts in different functions. Your child might have a seventh-grade brain for reading but a nursery-school brain for social relationships, all at the age of eight. Often this uneven development is built into the child's genetic pattern, so that little Jimmy is a late bloomer in language, just like his father was. Asymmetrical development sometimes evens out as a child develops, but often kids with asymmetrical development will need help to support the weaker areas, such as language or reading or learning to self-regulate. Sometimes certain skills are so weak that they do not respond well to interventions.

When your child has been diagnosed, you will need to take into account all the facets of the disorder and retrain yourself to communicate with him or her in the most effective way. If your child has an auditory processing disorder, yelling at or nagging him because he won't follow verbal directions is not going to accomplish anything aside from making you both feel terrible. It is a complex condition about which you, your child, and your family will need to educate yourselves. The way to cut down on the incidents that make you feel angry is to learn which methods of communication work best with your particular child.

Despite your best intentions, there will still be times when you and your child don't connect. When atypical children are feeling needy, they ask for help from their parents in ways that are not always verbal or socially appropriate. A stressed-out child who processes information differently can stress out the parent. Sometimes the child acts out or becomes withdrawn. Or aggressive. Or sad. Or isolated. Or has no friends.

Whether a child is struggling physically, emotionally, or socially, the attuned parent will hear the child's cry for help. It can be useful to ask yourself a few questions on a regular basis: What signal is my child sending me? Am I missing anything in this picture? Do I need to become a more attuned parent and control my emotions better? I don't think there is a parent on the planet who wouldn't benefit from this type of periodic self-reflection.

When You Are Not Angry but Your Partner Is

Not every parent of an atypical child goes through the anger phase, but I'd be willing to bet that even if you are not feeling bitter or blameful about your child's condition, someone close to you—your spouse, your parent, another family member—is. That was the case with Bill, the grandpa at the beginning of this chapter. He and his wife, Leslie, were the guardians of their five-year-old grandson, Ryan, who had high-functioning autism. This can be a tricky diagnosis for caretakers because high-functioning autistics can sometimes pass for neurotypical children, and at other times they may decompensate without warning. *Decompensation* means the deterioration of assumed self-control of mastered skills. With high-functioning autism, it means the child suddenly is not able to "compensate for," or handle, factors such as stress, fatigue, or too much stimulation. Because these children may handle their surroundings fairly well much of the time, it is easy to ignore or dismiss if you are not fully informed. Clearly, this is what was occurring with Ryan's grandfather.

During one of Ryan's office visits, I asked the boy to finish this sentence: "My grandma thinks I am . . ."

"Smart," Ryan answered in a soft voice.

"And what about this one," I continued. "My grandpa thinks I am . . ."

Ryan looked down, afraid and sad.

"Do you want to finish the sentence, Ryan?"

"No, I don't want to," he said, and proceeded to list the names of his favorite dinosaurs.

Leslie was attentive and patient with her grandson. She understood that children could have quirks and idiosyncrasies, and although she was concerned about Ryan's odd behavior, she didn't blame him for it. She wanted to help him. Bill did not share Leslie's tolerance or her nuanced thinking. Rather, he saw the world in black and white. "Children are treated with kid gloves these days," he said, "and that's why they've got all these weird problems—like Ryan." Bill told me that when he was a boy, "we fell into line or else. My dad had a belt hanging in the closet and he wasn't afraid to use it. None of this namby-pamby coddling!"

During one of our first appointments, it was clear that Bill was exasperated and angry. "I'm sick of this!" he said. "What's with this kid, anyway? He hates to get his hands dirty and he's scared of all these normal things. I refuse to put up with it anymore!" Bill was stuck in the absolute thinking of the anger response; he was so angry that he didn't want to deal with the gray areas of this condition. Absolute thinking is common when people are angry; when the emotions take over your critical thinking skills, the fine-tuned nuances of situations disappear and become vigorously "clear" in absolute terms. Thus, when a parent snaps, they will sound like Bill, speaking in absolutes with the emotional conviction of one who is absolutely sure of their position. Yet underneath anger is uncertainty, anxiety, and fear. In Bill's case, fear of the financial burden was not the least of it.

After assessing Ryan and informing Bill and Leslie that their grandson would benefit from speech therapy, social skills training, and possibly a special school, Bill blew up. "No way! That's absurd. And all that so-called treatment is going to cost a fortune!"

Bill not only condemned his wife for being too understanding and spending too much time with Ryan, he also took his anger out on the boy. When I asked Bill about his temper, he relied on a common refrain often cited by angry parents: "Why, when I was a child . . ." Bill replied that when he was a child, no one paid attention to him the way Leslie did with Ryan. "She's a helicopter parent, and she's ruining him. She should let him figure things out on his own—let him learn the hard way."

It was no surprise that Ryan was scared of his volatile grandfather. Although Bill loved his grandson, anger was his most visible emotion. And Ryan and Leslie were not the only targets. During parent-teacher conferences, doctor visits, and with every specialist who worked with Ryan, Bill's rage spewed forth. He ranted that "so-called professionals" were ruining his boy and that he was the only one who knew how to deal with him. His preferred treatment was talking to his grandchild with harsh words and expecting more of him than was feasible.

This was a family on the brink of falling apart due to Bill's anger. Yet underneath that anger was anxiety. Bill's explosive outbursts were reactions to his inner fears about his grandson's strange behavior. Because he was not only antagonistic toward the professionals involved in this case but also heavily guarded emotionally, it took months before Bill was able to break through the wall of anger to his underlying panic.

Helping Others Acknowledge Their Anger

If you are living with an angry person in your household, you must know how destructive their anger is to everyone around them.

Your first responsibility is to protect your child. There are parents who don't want to deal with the fact that their child is potentially being hurt by their partner's anger. In most of these cases, the quieter parent endures the outbursts, downplaying the problem and hoping the storm will pass. Too often, this parent cannot fully shield the child. If this is you, please listen carefully: *This must stop.* You cannot hope to diffuse your spouse's anger when he or she is in a rage. But your child comes first. This difficult situation must be rectified, even if it means taking your child and leaving the home until the angry person agrees to anger management therapy. There is no way that ongoing anger is not affecting your child and your family.

We mentioned at the beginning of this chapter that many parents don't realize how angry they are or how hostile they appear to others. Even if they do, they may justify their behavior. I have found that a simple technique, videotaping them for a few minutes, can sometimes shock these people to their senses. Then—and this is important—show them the video later, when they are not angry. At that point you can say, "Is this who you want to be?"

Your child comes first.

Once the other person has been made aware of their anger and acknowledges that they want to change, there are a number of options. He or she can go to therapy, to anger management classes, or can try one of the techniques we mention at the end of this chapter. Your responsibility is not to solve the other person's anger issues. It is to protect your child and alert the other person to the fact that he or she has a problem. You can support them in their efforts to deal with it, but ultimately you cannot do it for them. The good news is that most parents deeply care about their child and want to be the best parent they can be. When they become aware of just how angry they really act and how that affects their child, that can be the impetus to change.

Bill's Turnaround

Bill, Ryan's grandfather, probably didn't realize when he and his family came to my office that he too would be receiving therapy. Bill was unprepared for a child who was atypical and he struggled with what this meant for him. Did it reflect on his ability as a caretaker? Did it mean he was a failure? What did it mean in terms of having to shell out extra resources to help this child? And why was this child so different? Bill had never articulated these questions, even to himself. He was a man of few words but a strong sense of pride in his identity as a caretaker and family man.

It was not easy to confront Bill or to change his habitual pattern of response, but Leslie insisted and took him to see a therapist who specializes in anger treatment. There, with Leslie at his side, Bill learned that his angry way of responding was seriously affecting his relationship with Leslie and hurting his little grandson. Bill was visibly moved when it finally sunk in. "I didn't mean . . . I'm just trying . . . It's such a hard situation, and I'm so tired."

Ryan's condition had made Bill feel helpless, and he had no experience trusting other people to do what was best for his grandson. Together, he and Leslie worked on supporting each other in roles neither of them had anticipated, but in which both very much wanted to succeed. Bill agreed to learn more about autism, and he even began attending a support group with Leslie for parents of autistic children. He continued on his own in therapy to work on learning nonaggressive ways to express his disappointment and fear of the future, and on developing a sense of optimism. Ryan's therapist helped Bill develop fun activities Ryan and Bill could enjoy together. Bill and Leslie arranged for a weekly date night so that their lives wouldn't just be about Ryan. In about six months, the family was able to change their dynamic and move closer to the goal—acceptance.

Biological Challenges Underneath
the Anger Response

Bill's angry response to his grandson's condition was influenced by a number of factors, including his own upbringing and personality, as well as a need to perceive Ryan as a positive reflection of himself. Another factor is more physiologically based.

Over the last several decades, research on brain function has focused on identifying areas of the brain that are responsible for various behaviors. The hormones that affect behavior are also at play. More research is now being devoted to how specific hormones and neurotransmitters (chemicals that transmit nerve impulses across synapses) create moods and emotional states, traits, and behaviors, regardless of where in the brain this is happening. The hormones that are associated with aggression in both sexes are the androgens. This category includes testosterone, DHEA (dehydroepiandrosterone), and androstenedione.[7] Testosterone is considered "the male hormone" because it is estimated that men produce more than ten times as much of it as women.[8] That's not to say that women can't be angry or aggressive. In fact, testosterone is a necessary hormone for both men and women, providing energy, libido, and zest for life. But it can propel some into impulsive or angry behavior if left unchecked.

Of course, we can't blame aggression on hormones alone; people need to be responsible for their actions. But hormones do play a very important role in our perception of reality and our reactions to the events in our lives. If it was only hormones controlling our emotions, most people would be flying off the handle every time something doesn't go their way, instead of controlling their aggressive impulses and remaining calm, even with a biological predisposition toward more aggressive responses.

Biology also provides us with calming and loving hormones. The magic hormone is oxytocin. Estrogen increases the release and distribution of oxytocin, particularly when a woman gives birth. Oxytocin may significantly influence prosocial behavior and may be the evolutionary source of caregiving.[9] In fact, researchers have tried injecting a chemical version of oxytocin into the noses of people with autism to see if it will bring about the reciprocity and social-emotional caring that come naturally when oxytocin levels are high. There is some early research to suggest that this is a potential future treatment for some types of issues. There is even research showing that oxytocin is lower in people with autism, and that men who are not involved in nurturing relationships may have lower levels of oxytocin.[10]

As soon as a woman gives birth, and while she is breastfeeding, her body produces a surge of oxytocin. It's nature's way of assuring that new mothers will be loving and empathic toward their offspring. The baby's touch, smell, and skin-to-skin bonding all increase levels of oxytocin. The repercussions are tremendous; in essence, the female brain changes into a highly protective and nurturing brain. Even women who work full-time have a brain overload of oxytocin (which creates many internal conflicts in terms of returning to work). The oxytocin surge is so powerful that mothers can become overwhelmingly defensive and even aggressive when it comes to protecting their babies.[11]

Fathers can be filled with oxytocin too as they engage with their newborn and older children. Research has demonstrated that the oxytocin spike can occur in all nurturing and physical relationships—when a parent nurtures a child, when friends exhibit caring behaviors toward one another, and by touching or being touched. Even rubbing someone's skin or petting a dog increases oxytocin.[12] It is sometimes called the love hormone because you feel much more loving toward others when you have an abundance of oxytocin in your system.[13] That is one reason fathers are encouraged to begin skin-to-skin bonding with their babies as soon as possible—the experience of being a hands-on father increases hormones for nurturing.[14] In my practice,

I see a fair number of gay male partners who have adopted children and who are tremendously nurturing. However, all parents must struggle with managing their emotional responses and adapting more appropriate and nurturing responses, no matter how our biological makeup may try to tell us differently.

Biology Isn't Destiny—In Fact, Destiny Can Change Biology

It was Freud who wrote that biology is destiny, referring to his belief that women's personalities and behaviors are entirely due to their biological makeup. We now emphatically know that this isn't true, that our biology isn't the only factor affecting our behavior, thoughts, or personalities. In fact, what we now know to be true is that *we can alter our own biochemical makeup* based on our behavior, practices, and beliefs. Not only is biology not destiny, in fact, *destiny can become your biology.* Your behaviors actually can create significant changes in your brain! Research has found that our brains are experience-dependent, and that your actions, decisions, and what you tell your brain to do, even the relationships that you are in, actually change the architecture of your brain. Neuroscientists refer to this as *neuroplasticity.* This means that the brain can be affected by environment, interpersonal relationships, and events. It is important to know that we can change our own brains. Just as you can improve your golf swing or learn hip-hop dance, you can also train your brain to develop patience, compassion, empathy, and kindness. And whether it is the golf swing or compassion that you are working on, your brain starts to rewire itself. We are not at the mercy of our genetically based brain wiring or our hormones. Knowing this can help you ward off feelings of helplessness or lack of control, which tend to trigger anger. You may not be able to control your child's condition as much as you would wish, but one thing is for sure: You can control your reactions and your response to your child. And as you start to control your responses and cultivate more positive and healthy coping mechanisms, your brain will change right along with you and soften your shortcomings into positive changes. This goes a step further: The field of interpersonal neurobiology has demonstrated that making personal changes will positively affect those around you. As you build internal levels of compassion, self-control, resilience, and positive attitudes, your work affects those around you, creating larger and larger concentric circles. As Daniel J. Siegel writes, "No one is an island; we are the outcomes of a dance of connection of where we've been . . . where we are now . . . and where we empower ourselves to create a future that we can actively shape."[15] From this perspective, it may not be our fault that we are wired with a tendency toward feeling angry, but it is our responsibility to use our awareness and intentions to refine our biological nature. "Inspire to rewire" is a goal of interpersonal neurobiology; we can rewire our brains, we can change automatic angry responses into calm, focused, and loving behaviors. We do this for our own good, for the good of our children, our relationships, and ultimately for our community. Changing your biology can change the destiny of both yourself as well as others.

Composed in Public, Angry at Home

I often marvel at how serenely some parents receive the news that their child has a learning difference or developmental challenge. Utterly composed, they take in my assessment and suggestions, agree to the advised protocol, and graciously tell me they look forward to their child's next visit. *Wow*, I say to myself, *that was easy.*

Then the same parents return the following week or a few months later with a wholly altered demeanor. Visibly anxious and upset, it is clear that their child's situation has caused the couple marital turmoil. They're angry about the diagnosis, and the target for their anger is each other. With professionals, they are reasonable and co-operative; but with each other, behind closed doors, criticism and accusations take over.

Such was the case with Jen and Leo. Their son, Nick, was adopted as an infant. His background was unknown, but at birth he received a positive toxicology screen, indicating that he had been exposed prenatally to drugs. His parents were troubled by much of his behavior.

The first time they came to see me they couldn't have been more gracious—and grateful to me for sorting out the mystery involving their son. After assessing six-year-old Nick, I determined that he met criteria for several diagnoses. Among them were ADHD, auditory processing disorder, developmental coordination disorder, and learning delays. He also had some unusual memory processing problems. I had a lot of interventions to offer them, and I was impressed with how easily they both went along with the program. "That sounds good, we'll do whatever it takes," Leo assured me. Several days later they had already contacted the specialist to whom I had referred them. Again, I marveled at how unusual it was for parents to get right on it and to be so efficient.

But what seemed to be a smooth acceptance eroded at home, once the information about their son sank in and they had the privacy to thrash it out between themselves. They soon entered into a phase where they each reacted differently. Leo focused entirely on his son and how to fix the issues, but he ended up ignoring his wife's needs in the few spare hours each night that they had together. Leo often noticed Jen crying in the middle of the night, but he ignored that too, thinking she would get over it. Jen did not read the report about her son and became obsessed with housecleaning. Leo soon began to snap at Jen for not focusing on priorities, and his criticism sparked full-scale arguing. The couple drifted apart: Jen withdrew, and Leo became more intent on "fixing" Nick and upset at the loss of Jen's emotional presence. Evenings became times of bickering, nit-picking, and each adult withdrawing to his or her corner of the house after they put Nick to bed. They did not take the time to deal with the deterioration in their relationship and eventually they separated.

The flip-flop in Jen and Leo's response to distressing news about their son has a neuropsychological explanation. During the workday we tend to shelve our primitive emotions in favor of optimizing our cognitive efficiency. We're in thinking and reasoning mode. So if parents walk into my office straight from their workaday world and receive a report about their child, they're all geared up cognitively and ready to tackle the issues. They're going to hear information and respond by saying something like, "Okay, that makes a lot of sense—let's do it." And they'll likely stay in that mode until their defenses are down. That usually happens in the evenings when they are tired from their long days, the kids get cranky, and the household workload intensifies. Parents will continue long into the night taking care of all the demands, and sooner or later, the cognitive overload hits the overactive limbic system and boom!—the emotions, which have been lying dormant and pent up all day, will surge forward, seeking release. Something will snap, usually at someone in the home or themselves. Yelling, drinking, bitter arguments, or despondency may be the result, along with insomnia.

For most adults, things start to unravel emotionally before bedtime. By 3:00 a.m., your defenses are down and the "worry brain" wakes up. Sleep consists of your brain and body going through an automatic self-repair process, wherein all circuits actively troubleshoot possible issues going on in the body or mind. It is now that leftover problems will resurface—a sore wrist, a conflict at work, or your child's most recent challenge. Rumination, anger, helplessness, shame, embarrassment, or despair can become most intense in the middle of the night. As you worry, you lose precious hours of sleep, which leads to being tired the next day and having fewer emotional resources. It's a vicious circle. F. Scott Fitzgerald observed, "In the dark night of the soul it is always three o'clock in the morning." Nobody knows this better than parents of children who are struggling. It is only a matter of time before the very logical, linear, "Yes, let's get with the program" attitude transforms into worry, fear, anger, and blame. The brain can only compartmentalize thoughts and feelings for so long before it seeks to reintegrate. Mindful integration of your feelings by processing them during the daytime, talking them out, even with yourself, helps you stay integrated and balanced. Being aware of the emotional and physiological forces that lead to anger and blame can help you manage them. When you're in workday mode you can come up with a game plan to deal with the minefields waiting at home. The section at the end of this chapter and the resources at the back of the book will give you some pointers.

Can Anger Ever Be a Good Thing?

With increased awareness and practice, angry feelings can be turned into productive actions. Anger can be a source of energy and motivation, as we saw earlier when Maggie and Kevin demanded that their son's school honestly assess the boy's progress. Many activists who have worked hard to change government policies or researchers who are involved in finding medical solutions or doctors who provide excellent care have, at their source, felt anger over social inequity, poor medical conditions among less fortunate, or the devastating conditions in third world countries. There are countless examples of people who are angry at the way things are and become determined to help change things. This "anger" is actually a source of motivational power that generates positive productivity. Even with marathon runners, there is anecdotal evidence to back up the belief that anger over prior unsuccessful marathon races can provide emotional fuel for runners and lead to improved times. Referred to as "race-day rage," the anger-as-motivator approach has also been described as the warrior mentality, a killer instinct, or a reptilian brain response.

Sometimes a rush of anger can be invigorating because it injects energy into your brain so that you can fix the problem at hand. When this happens, anger can be harnessed for the common good. You may be angry at society for its mistreatment of the disadvantaged, minorities, or women, and channel that anger into a persuasive demonstration or a nonprofit group to improve human rights. We might even say that the polio vaccine was created because people were angry at the disease for causing so much pain. Scientists transformed that outrage into action. So it is possible for anger to be a beneficial energy source that springs from a deep internal well.

In the context of a parent's struggle with his or her child's condition, anger can lead to creative solutions ("We're angry that our child has this problem—and we're committed to finding remedies"). Essentially, parental anger in this instance is a survival mechanism. In that sense it is a positive stage in the progress toward acceptance, because it means that you are not denying your child's condition, but rather you are making a move. You are declaring to yourself and perhaps to others, "I'm angry! And I'm going to pull my child and my family out of this morass!"

Many parents have told me that the times they get angry (not superhot, just hot enough) are when they develop their best plans. When you are superhot, you need to slow down and do some deep breathing. It is never—I repeat, *never*—the time to act. Instead, take a walk outside. Take a break and retreat to the bathroom for a few minutes. Don't let your anger hijack your thinking brain to the point of destruction. Give your brain time to process and reorganize the information. Many people use mindfulness techniques for exactly this purpose. (See the suggestions at the end of this chapter.)

You do not have to practice mindfulness in order to conquer your angry impulses, but it sure helps. Mindfulness does not mean spending hours in some shrine meditating. It can be but a moment periodically during your day. Focusing on the present moment, becoming aware of what you are thinking and feeling, breathing deeply, and noticing the sensations in your body will give you enough mental space to cool down and choose the high road. That way, instead of causing you to lash out, your anger will fuel your problem-solving creativity and give you the courage to act on your proactive plan instead of lurching into a destructive reaction.

All that being said, the pressing problem for most parents is not harnessing their productive anger but managing their destructive anger. Parents, especially those with atypical kids, need anger-management strategies they can adapt as their child grows and changes.

Summing Up: The Awful Price of Anger

In this chapter, we have learned that anger is normal and an important basic emotion necessary for survival. Anger can be an activating force and a motivator. In prehistoric times, when the struggle for life was so risky, anger served as a call to action to protect oneself and one's family. In modern times, anger can be activated when our path to a goal or something we hold dear is blocked. Frustration and anger make us want to force things, retaliate, or reclaim control by aggression. As we saw, anger seeks a target, which is why we blame others or ourselves when we become angry.

Although the original goal of anger was self-protection and survival, it is quite evident that anger is often damaging. In the case of parents who are learning to come to terms with their children's differences, anger is a phase that usually comes directly after denial. After moving out of the numbness, reality awakens the protective momma bear and the initial instinct is to push back and shout, "Leave us alone or I will destroy you!"

Although anger may serve some purpose, no one should be ignorant of the havoc it can wreak on families and children. Here is what we know:

- Atypical families have a much higher rate of divorce.
- Anger causes verbal and physical abuse, with long-term repercussions for the child.
- Research shows that even sleeping infants are affected by their parents' fighting.
- Anger often leads to divorce, which is damaging on many levels. The caretaking parent is usually left with less financial and personal support, resulting in worse care for the child, a more stressed-out parent, and a cascade of other negative outcomes.
- Angry outbursts in front of others (family, friends) can cause them to back away, resulting in the family being even more isolated.
- Children growing up in angry households are less likely to thrive.
- Children who see angry parents are likely to model angry coping mechanisms themselves.
- Anger or hostility isolates parents from the very services that they desperately need. When an angry parent confronts a teacher or doctor, these professionals tend to shy away from the conflict.

Anger and blame can destroy a family if it goes on too long or fails to dissipate and give way to understanding and the pursuit of solutions. Your goal is to deal with your child's problems, not point the finger. Again, your son or daughter's condition is because of a dysfunction in the brain, not the result of faulty caretaking or mismanaged schools. Lashing out in anger is understandable but ultimately counterproductive.

Your child needs to be protected from inappropriate ongoing anger, and so does your whole family. Think of your child's condition as a wobbly wooden suspension bridge that sways when you walk across it. Your anger (or your partner's anger) is like the guy who stomps across the bridge making everyone else on it lose their footing. If you're not mindful of the fact that it's a shaky bridge to begin with, everyone on it can lose their balance and fall over.

I tell parents all the time: "You are not the cause of your child's condition. But you can sure make it worse. You've got to become mindful of that shaky bridge. If you understand where your anger is coming from and take steps to heal it, you can pass through the anger phase without harming those you love."

Anger Management Techniques

So here is the truth. While feelings of anger, hostility, frustration, and blame are natural emotions along the parenting journey, you have a choice. You can choose to stay stuck in your emotional swamp or you can decide to shift your energy in a more positive direction. Just as angry emotions cause larger ripples in the pond, so do positive emotions. You can choose to say, "It sucks and I hate that we don't know exactly what is wrong with our child and the school system is so unhelpful and no one wants to play with my kid and my kid is driving me crazy!" Or you can work on your feelings to become a conscious, active player in your situation, instead of feeling like a victim.

So be proactive and ask yourself, *Do I want to live in an environment of anger?* There is so much anger around us, from road rage to violence on TV and violence in the news. Do you really want to be part of that? There is another way. I invite you to try the following exercises, which can help you understand, avert, or tame your angry episodes. Please note that this book is not an anger-management text or a substitute for professional counseling. The techniques that follow are specifically aimed for people going through a phase of anger as part of their coming to grips with the fact that their child has a disorder. There is a difference between that and having chronic problems with anger. However, regardless of the reason or duration of your anger, I urge you to seek the help of a therapist if you feel that it is escalating or is already out of control.

Breathe

> *Just breathe. Ten tiny breaths . . . Seize them. Feel them. Love them.*
>
> —K. A. Tucker, *Ten Tiny Breaths*

Taking two or three deep breaths periodically during the day releases pent-up tension. It might seem too simple to be an effective antidote for anger, yet deep breathing has been found to be invaluable in developing a relaxation response. You can't be angry and relaxed at the same time, right? Just breathe in . . . and out . . . in . . . and out . . . A few minutes of breathing slowly and deeply takes the zing out of a potentially toxic situation. It clears the mind and allows you to see that there are answers to your challenges. When you feel that there are answers, your anger will loosen its grip as your optimism builds.

Use the STOP Method to Calm Down Quickly

This technique was first developed as part of mindfulness-based stress reduction (MBSR) training and written about more fully by Dr. Elisha Goldstein, a leader in the psychology of meditation and author of *The Now Effect*.

Stop. Take a moment to step into the pause of life, training the ability to slow down rather than rushing into an angry retort or aggressive action. Your hand is on the doorknob of your child's room and your impulse is to rush in and let him know exactly how angry you are that he didn't clean his room, do his homework, or go to bed.

Take a deep breath. Slow down, take several more deep breaths, and try to regulate your breathing. If you like, you can extend this for a few more moments, noticing your body naturally breathing "in" and "out." Can you notice how distraught you are? Is it really about your child or is it something else? How has your day gone? Are you seeking release of stress through an irrational moment? Breathe. Don't move for a moment. Just breathe.

Observe. How does your body feel? What type of thoughts are flooding through your mind? Why are you so angry? Who are you about to take it out on? Do they (or do you) deserve it?

Chances are you have had a bad day apart from your child. Feel compassion wash over you for a moment as you give yourself a mental hug. Say to yourself, "May you be well."

Proceed. Take a few more deep breaths and proceed by asking yourself, "What is the most important thing to do right now?" Allow the answer to be that wise voice that leads you to a more peaceful and regulated solution.

When You Feel Yourself Boiling Over, Call for Backup

It's so important to notice your internal emotional signals when your kettle is starting to boil. Don't ignore it. Take a time-out. Have a code word you can use with your partner that automatically buys you fifteen minutes of alone time to cool down if you feel your anger swelling up. If you're a single parent, have a close neighbor or two agree to take your child for fifteen minutes in these instances. You will be surprised at how much fifteen minutes of "chill time" buys you. It's worth having a conversation with your partner or understanding neighbor on a day where everything is going well. Make it clear just how important this is for the well-being of your family. Prepare for the next inevitable meltdown. It will happen. And you will be ready.

Observe Yourself for One Day

Take a clear look at yourself. Spend one day observing yourself as if from a video camera. Be aware of your feelings and also of your facial expressions and body language. (Hint: Quick peeks in the mirror might surprise you!) Where do you hold your tension? What is your anger pattern? Do you let it build up until you explode? Are you constantly overcritical? Is your tone of voice aggressive and challenging? (Hint: Record a conversation and play it back later.)

Take a Risk: Ask Others

Ask those close to you if they think you are angry too often and what they observe. You may not agree with them, but your willingness to have this conversation can open a stream of communication that might surprise you. As an extra incentive, remember that children learn by imitation. Modeling good anger-management techniques will foster good habits in your kids.

Reality Check: What Makes You Angry and Why?

What triggers your anger? Is it really because your child is different? What does that bring up for you? Why is anger a frequent response? Write down the situations that are most likely to trigger an angry outburst and note how that interferes with your relationships. Do any of the following strike you as being one of your personal emotional triggers?

- Being treated unfairly or disrespectfully
- Threats to your security or the security of your child
- Threats to your self-image
- Fear of being out of control

- Fear of the unknown
- Unmet expectations—deep disappointment

Check out your irrational beliefs: Anger often makes us assume things that may or may not be true. For example, your anger may fire up when you're in a meeting with your child's teacher—it seems like she's judging you and talking down to you. Ask yourself, do you know this is true? Be open to the idea that you may be overreacting. Notice the specific things your children or other people do that irritate you, and ask yourself what might be coloring your perceptions and triggering your anger. Noticing is learning. What do you think needs to be changed? How will you do it?

Create a Game Plan for Your Worst Triggers

Now that you are aware of the events or actions that trigger your anger, create a game plan for dealing with the worst of the incidents. One very common scenario is the parent who walks in the door after work and is immediately besieged by needy children. Parents have told me that several things trigger their ire: instantly being jumped on without so much as a hello, being bombarded with demands ("I'm hungry!" "Where were you?"), or complaints ("She hit me!"), and not having a mental moment to transition from working person to parent.

I have often advised parents that the following game plan works for improving the daily homecoming. First, at a time other than the arrival, sit down with your children and partner and calmly tell them how you are feeling: "You know what we need to change? When you jump on me the minute I walk in the door and don't even say hello or ask how my day was. Can we change that? Let's practice." They then do a practice run, with the children behaving as requested. This should be done in the spirit of fun, yet with the understanding that it's not a game—you mean it. I realize it can be difficult to train special-needs kids, but teaching them empathy and basic manners is fundamental to their ability to get along in the world. Learning to ask about your day is an excellent beginning in developing empathy for your child, as well.

With the training in place (you may have to repeat it a number of times), you can enact the other half of game plan: mentally preparing yourself for the trigger situation. For coming home, this means allowing yourself a few minutes in the car (down the block, if necessary) to sit, compose yourself, anticipate what's ahead, and envision how you will respond.

The same basic strategy works in all trigger situations. Preplan your events. First consider what the other person (doctor, relative, teacher, your spouse) is likely to do that may push your buttons. Then think about what you can ask them to do differently, in a diplomatic and nonhostile way. For example, with a doctor you might prepare a list of questions and preface your visit with, "I sometimes end up feeling frustrated after these meetings because I can't totally follow what you're saying. I know your time is limited, but is it okay if I interrupt and ask questions if I need to?" Before your meeting, take some deep breaths, focus, anticipate what the doctor might say, and review your list of questions.

You can see that the operative word in game plan is *plan*. Be proactive. Anticipate your reactions, communicate your wishes, and alter your own behavior to change the outcome of the situation.

Blame and Reframe: Changing an Angry Mindset

Having a game plan for situations that trigger you is a good way to start redirecting your angry responses. Changing an angry mindset takes a different type of work. In these cases, we have a belief that evolved from a specific situation and our initial response to it. That

BLAMING	REFRAMING
We have just been told that my son has a learning disability. I'm in shock because I thought he was doing fine. I think it's because my husband and I got divorced when our son was little, and he was traumatized. I loathe my husband for walking out on us and ruining our son's life. I'm filled with hateful venom.	Divorce is never easy, but it is unlikely that it has created a learning disability in our son. Despite the fact that I feel angry and abandoned by my husband, it is important that he and I maintain consistent conditions for learning in both our homes. Maybe we can share a tutor or agree on the amount of time our son spends studying. I will make sure I have enough emotional support as I continue to be the best single parent I can be under difficult circumstances.
My wife worked all the time when she was pregnant and also when our daughter was an infant. Our little girl is autistic. How can I not blame my wife? She's the mother and she ignored our baby. I'm so furious!	My wife's earlier behavior infuriates me. But there is no evidence that it caused our daughter's autism. Scientists do not know all the causes of autism, but they believe it might be a disruption of normal brain development early in the fetal stage. The theory that parental practices are responsible for autism has long been disproved. My wife is in pain over this like I am. Isolating myself from my wife because of this misplaced anger may lead to depression. Anger in the house will also be bad for my daughter. We both need to take a look at how much time we spend with our daughter right now and see if we need to increase time with her.

BLAMING	REFRAMING
Our neighborhood is full of snobby mothers who have no idea about how much I suffer because my child is different. They're so smug and brag all the time about how advanced their kids are. They have no idea how much I despise them and their cute little perfect geniuses.	I'm angry that other moms do not have to go through what I do. I hate to admit it, but I know I'm overly sensitive and envious. I want them to know what it's like. Maybe I can get someone from an organization that represents my child's condition to speak at the next PTA meeting. That speaker might be able to help me tell the other parents what my needs are. If I reach out, maybe someone will reach back.
Our daughter's teacher is just terrible! She's young and doesn't know how to teach, so our daughter fell behind this year. She is so incompetent and I want to smack her! Someone should fire her! I can't wait to talk to the principal about her at the school picnic.	It's true that she's young and hasn't been trained in special ed. But it's also true that our daughter likes this teacher. I'm frustrated and anxious because we're not sure our daughter's needs are being met at this school. The fact is that we may have to find help for her outside the classroom. Atypical kids often require specialized teaching methods. I'll call the teacher to discuss how we can work together to get my daughter what she needs.
Our doctor is so impatient with us. He talks down to us, smiles patronizingly and gives us too much jargon. I'm freaking out, and he's a smug jerk.	I'm angry at our doctor, but I need more information from him. I'll schedule an appointment without our child and I will bring a list of the questions I want answered. If he can't answer them, I will ask for a referral to a specialist. If that doesn't work, I will find a new doctor.

BLAMING	REFRAMING
I'm a terrible parent. Every day I yell at my son—he's driving me crazy! I think he is doing this on purpose to make me mad. I feel like throttling him when I see him after work.	The level of anger I feel toward my child is frightening me. I understand that he cannot control himself, but I'm still furious with him. I know I need help, but I'm scared and ashamed. I've got to think about my son and family first and call a therapist. *Note: Anytime a parent gets this angry at his or her child, it's a red flag. Please seek treatment immediately. A child with an atypical condition is at risk here. Children cannot control themselves like adults can. Counseling is available and will help you become a better parent.*
The school meeting is midway through and I feel myself losing it. These people just don't get it. I'm going to tell them exactly how I feel about their coldhearted bureaucratic 'tudes!	I need to take a break from this meeting. To the administration, this is just another child. Their emotions are not on the line like mine are. I'll go outside, practice my deep breathing, and take a short walk around the schoolyard. This meeting isn't a make-or-break moment. *Note: If it is make-or-break, ask to reschedule the meeting for another time, when you can bring in an advocate to help you present your case in a more effective manner.*

belief may have taken root recently or it may be longstanding. By looking at it dispassionately, you can reframe the blame. The key to reframing is getting valid information and taking action. In other words, use your thinking brain to calm your emotional brain and redirect your energy. The chart beginning on page 121 gives examples of blame/reframe situations common to a lot of the parents I know. For your own purposes, keep a journal of your angry thoughts and feelings. Later, when you've cooled down, go back and try to reframe the situation. Include other people's points of view and facts, even if you hate to admit to them.

Boost Your Tolerance Level

In addition to the strategies outlined above, it's wise to have a self-care routine that will increase your level of tolerance for the situations that trigger your anger. This can be tricky, because the very things that make a person resistant to meltdowns are scarce in the lives of most parents: nutritious meals, exercise, and enough sleep. We tend to see these as luxuries, but they are the fuel that enables you to be a tolerant and loving parent. To help protect against angry outbursts, you must give your body what it needs to function better. Abiding by the following guidelines can improve your mood and resilience:

1. **Eat a high-protein breakfast.** No sugar-packed smoothies or coffee and a granola bar. The old standard works well: eggs, whole-wheat toast, fruit such as apple or banana, and bacon or sausage if you're so inclined.

2. **Notice how caffeinc affects you.** I'm not telling you to give up coffee, but do notice how it makes you feel. If you're too caffeinated, it can jettison all your good intentions and push you to a massive emotional overreaction.

3. **Love the body you're in, but keep it moving.** Even if you do a good deal of walking every day, notice how you move. You can walk in a tense, hunched-up way, thinking about what you need

to do next, or you can swing your arms and breathe in the air and use it to get in a few moments of exhilarating movement. If you can regularly walk with a friend, it is very therapeutic—even (or especially) if you don't talk about your child at all. Your walk can be a time of respite, when you can reliably think and converse about something besides your child as part of your self-care routine. This is not the time to berate yourself for not hitting the gym or not fitting into your old clothes. Walking is a feel-good exercise, designed to boost your endorphin level and discharge negative internal energy in a positive manner.

4. **Get enough sleep.** If you are not getting enough sleep, it sets up a pattern of poor coping behavior. Lack of exposure to natural sunlight during the daytime hours, too little movement during the day, and ingesting "hidden" caffeine (in chocolate, Coke, or tea, for example) too soon before bedtime may prevent you from sleeping soundly. To improve your sleep, try the following:

- Eliminate screen time before bed (the glare from computer screens, phones, and tablets has been found to disrupt natural circadian rhythms and keep you awake long into the night). I know you may feel left behind on your latest favorite TV series, but honestly, your sleep comes first.
- Engage in at least a bit of physical exercise during the day. Twenty minutes of heart-pumping, adrenaline-rushing cardiovascular exercise does wonders. Break a sweat.
- Have a regular sleep routine that promotes relaxation. For my patients, I have developed a short yoga series of five stretches in five minutes to relax the body and get ready for sleep. I also recommend baths with Epsom or sea salts before bed as an alternative to showers.
- Use the love hormone, oxytocin. You can generate this feel-good chemical through physical touch (it doesn't have to be sex). Cuddle with your kid or your partner for a few minutes

before bedtime to get the oxytocin flowing. If you have a pet, you may get the same effect from spending some quality time with it. A study in Japan found that dog owners who played with their dogs and looked into their eyes for more than 2.5 minutes during the play session experienced a 20 percent increase in oxytocin.[16]

Anger-management strategies have a nice way of morphing into life-enhancing strategies. They will work to calm and center you in stressful moments, reinvigorate you, and increase your appreciation of the good times. When the anger and blame phase is just a memory, these tools will keep helping you improve your quality of life. And just in time! Because you will need your positive energy surge as you move into the bargaining phase.

CHAPTER FOUR

Bargaining and Seeking Solutions

"I Promise to Be the Best Mommy in the World"

Note to self:

Make appointment with new specialist.

Decide about which diet to try.

Note to principal of my son's school:

If I promise to get him a tutor every day, can he please stay in his class with his friends?

Note to doctor:

Who appointed you the world's greatest expert? I'm going to get another opinion!

Note to God:

If I promise to pray every morning, will you help my son?

—Denise, mother of an autistic ten-year-old

• • •

What exactly is bargaining and who is the bargaining parent? Everyone bargains to some extent. It's how we navigate through our complicated world, accepting some things, rejecting others, and compromising on most of it. Bargaining is a way to maintain a sense of control over life—if you can't get everything you want, at least you can get some of it. For parents of atypical kids, bargaining is an attempt to get back on track after the disorientation and emotional tumult of the denial and anger phases. If denial felt like a deer in headlights and anger felt like a momma bear protecting her cubs, the bargaining phase is akin to, well, the human being. Bargaining involves searching for solutions to your child's problems, which makes it the most cognitive phase and therefore the most human one we have discussed so far.

In the journey toward acceptance of the atypical child, the bargaining phase emerges when the anger simmers down to the extent that one can take reasonable—or somewhat reasonable—action. Bargaining takes the form of calm, focused, yet driven energy in the quest for a solution to the problem. Jaak Panksepp, in his seminal book on neuroscience, *The Archaeology of Mind*, discusses different systems of behavior that are common to all mammals. This type of bargaining behavior in parents best fits what Panksepp calls the *seeking system*: "[This system] allows animals to search for, find, and acquire all of the resources that are needed for survival."[1] Not only does the seeking system help animals survive, it also feels good. Panksepp describes the "positive, enthused affect" that may accompany a seeking behavior, as well as the depression and despair that follows if whatever is being sought is not found. He concludes, "It is now clear that when the system crashes, following repeated frustrations, people will feel depressed."[2] That is important to be aware of as you investigate various options for your child. Parents may vacillate between bargaining and depression many times during the course of raising a child, and it helps if you know that there is a back-and-forth rhythm between the two emotional states.

Parents who are still struggling to understand and help their atypical child will continue to experience a cascade of negative emotions. This is precisely the state, Panksepp notes, that triggers the seeking-system response. It feels good to be on the search for solutions. In fact, seeking in general can create so much positive feeling that some people continue to "seek" long after it is helpful. Parents who have an atypical child will have plenty of motivation to search for more information, alternative treatments, or state-of-the-art therapies. It's an intellectual exercise, triggered by underlying emotional needs, that feels productive. In many cases, it works. And sometimes, it doesn't.

Naturally, you will always want to be aware of promising new treatments. That aspect of seeking solutions is not a phase, it's part of parenting. Many thrilling scientific discoveries are being made regarding all sorts of disorders, so of course you want to stay on top of them. Later in the chapter, we'll explain how you can get help in monitoring new research concerning your child's condition. But you also need to be aware of the darker side of bargaining and seeking solutions—the side that has you up all night searching the Internet and blaming yourself if you can't uncover a cure, or trying questionable alternative therapies that may do nothing for your child except delay his or her access to more reliable treatments. You need to understand why you may be drawn to certain therapies and resistant to others, because when it comes to your child's care, you can't simply trust your gut. You've got to reasonably assess the options, and you must choose a team of doctors and therapists to trust.

Trusting the Standard of Care May
Feel Like a Leap of Faith

Standard of care refers to the recommended interventions that are accepted as "best practice" for a specific disorder. In many types of diagnoses, the standard of care may strike some parents as not being aggressive enough, or being too aggressive. Too medical, or too impersonal. Despite some parents' misgivings, the standard of care is based on years of research and field-tested results. So whenever a set of parents tells me that they've decided to ignore the standard of care in favor of untested theories, my heart breaks a little. We can't afford to lose one child to failure, discouragement, or unattended potential. When poorly tested but heavily marketed "treatments" make waves in the news or become popular in my neighborhood, I inwardly groan. It's true that we don't know everything about treating atypical children, and I will provide exciting stories about that shortly, but we do know a lot. And what we do know makes a difference.

One thing I believe all clinicians ought to make clear to parents when they explain the best standard of care for a child is that there are no guaranteed outcomes, even with evidence-based, time-tested treatments. A certain approach may be highly successful, but we cannot make ironclad promises. Anyone who does make such promises is probably lying. The fact is, parents need to learn to live with uncertainty. Once you have chosen a group of professionals and decided on a course of action, you need to take that leap of faith and trust your team and the process. This means accepting that you might not know for some time if the treatment will be successful. The anxiety of waiting makes some parents desperate, and they veer off the agreed-upon plan and start seeking alternative treatments. Other parents learn to live with the uncertainty and work with therapies that may not be perfect but are the best we currently have. These parents reconcile the urgent desire to "fix" their child with the patience required to follow through on the recommended treatments. This holds true for every atypical condition I can think of, whether it's ADHD, dyslexia, autism spectrum disorder, mood disorders, neurological disorders, genetic-based disorders, illness-based disorders, or brain injuries. The truth is that each child responds differently so we recommend a plan of action and reassess periodically.

Perseverance Pays Off

Pablo was a child with a lot going against him when I first met him. Born in Guatemala, he had come to this country with his family at the age of three, speaking only Spanish. His family struggled to become settled in the United States. On top of their other challenges, they soon noticed that Pablo was exhibiting behaviors that were profoundly different and disturbing. He was fascinated with fire by the age of four, had a history of trying to set fires, and was diagnosed with severe learning delays at age eight. He also had anxiety and obsessive-compulsive disorder that was so extreme there were nights he could only calm himself by sleeping in the closet with his dog.

Pablo's parents took him to as many specialists as they could. I was amazed that they found the energy and determination to keep going with their son. Behavior therapy, OCD clinic, learning remediation with an educational therapist five times a week, and psychotropic medications. And it wasn't only one medication; they tried several, and at times he was on three different medications and endured weight gain and insomnia as side effects. That's rough. But they stuck with their team of professionals, whom they deeply trusted. It was a long, slow haul with many starts and stops, small victories, and disappointing setbacks.

Pablo is now graduating from high school. He continues to struggle with some learning delays, but with the help of assistive technology, he is on his way to a college that provides accommodations. Most important, Pablo's behavior is under control. He understands his diagnoses and is constantly striving to improve himself. While he continues to be a work in progress (aren't we all?), he truly benefitted from parents who trusted their team and followed the prescribed regimen.

I highlight this story because people from different cultures are sometimes suspicious of local doctors. "Overmedication," they sniff.

"Back in our country, they know how to raise children." Parents who were born and raised in the same country as they are raising their child may also be skeptical of the pervasive culture's approach or what they perceive to be over-reliance on pharmaceuticals or lack of acceptance of alternative theories. Their wariness is understandable, and we'll explore it in a moment. But none of this should prevent parents from finding a core team of professionals they can relate to and trust. It's essential for the well-being of their child and parents.

The Neurobiology of Bargaining

Bargaining involves a kind of interplay between reason and emotion. In the bargaining phase, you are beginning to seek reasonable solutions, but you are still heavily influenced by your emotions—and how could you not be? Your child is grappling with a difficult condition, your entire family is deeply affected, you want to do what's best for your child, but you aren't sure which expert to trust and which diagnosis to believe. So your emotional brain is still on a roller coaster of fear, anger, confusion, anxiety. The roller coaster is starting to level off, but now the brain's response resembles a game of Ping-Pong—a back-and-forth exchange between emotion and reason.

An emotionally flooded brain is not an effective brain. When your prefrontal cortex is hijacked by your fears, worries, and rage, it is difficult to solve problems. In the bargaining phase, denial and anger have subsided a bit, and the prefrontal cortex is resuming control. Your prefrontal cortex is a problem-solving optimist: *There is a solution to be found, and we'll find it!*

Sometimes, though, the solutions your brain comes up with in the bargaining phase are not very well thought out. That is because there are still so many stressors, so many viewpoints to consider, so many choices, that the situation can become very complex. During this phase, the prefrontal cortex must sift through and process many emotionally fraught concerns, such as:

- What does this diagnosis really mean?
- How do I handle all these recommendations?
- How will my child adapt to this protocol versus that one?
- How will we afford it?
- How will all this affect our family?
- *What should I do?*

Eventually you will sort through the complexity and come up with some type of plan. It might be a simple plan, or a series of plans, or one bold experimental plan, but your brain is a solution seeker and it will try to settle on a plan of action. Remember too that the brain is always trying to maintain equilibrium between internally opposing forces. That's why a parent who reacts angrily to her child's diagnosis one week might be calm and rational the next week, after she has had a chance to digest the information.

Given the brain's need to solve problems and simplify the complex, and given the confusing array of issues facing the parent of a child with learning differences, you may go back and forth between emotions and reason until you land on one of the following "maybes":

- Maybe the psychologist's diagnosis is wrong and our child has a problem that's not so serious.
- Maybe there is a simple alternative to the list of treatments and special classes the therapist is suggesting.
- Maybe I can do some Internet research and find something that will work.
- Maybe if we spend more quality family time together, our daughter's autism will subside.
- Maybe that diet my neighbor suggested is the answer to our boy's ADHD.

- Maybe if I get rid of the TV, my son will read more and won't have dyslexia.
- Maybe if we just get her a tutor, our daughter will overcome her learning problems.
- Maybe my religious leader will have a solution.
- A lot of celebrities have had children with similar conditions. Maybe we should do what they did.

In the bargaining phase, a parent has come to accept that yes, something is different about his or her child and they had better find a solution, but he or she may not completely accept either the diagnosis or the suggested treatment. In the denial phase the self-talk was, *No way, this is not happening*, and in the anger phase it was, *Damn those so-called experts—I hate them all!* In the bargaining phase, the self-talk becomes more layered: *Maybe the experts are partially right, but I'm not sure. I need to figure this out on my own terms, because I don't like the label they're giving my kid or the treatment options they're suggesting. This diagnosis or treatment just doesn't feel right to me. And I don't like feeling out of control.*

Belief Perseverance: Why We Are Drawn to Certain Treatments and Reject Others

The bargaining phase is complicated because new alternative treatments are always cropping up, and many popular alternatives—such as homeopathic medicine, dietary adjustments, and "brain-based" techniques—are not necessarily backed by research-based efficacy studies. That's not to say they don't work. Sometimes they do. Still, I have found that it is common for some parents to trust alternative treatments more than traditional treatments that are validated by academic studies and recommended by professionals. Why is this?

Our brains hold a set of assumptions about who we are, and the news that our child is atypical may disrupt those assumptions. In response to this disruption of assumptions, our perception of reality becomes selective. We'll believe certain aspects of our child's diagnosis and reject others; we'll go along with certain scientifically proven recommendations and dispute others. Parents may be skeptical about doctors and other professionals in general—and understandably so, for a variety of reasons—whereas they're not skeptical about an unknown individual on the Internet who has posted an alternative therapy, or a celebrity who has written a book about an alternative treatment that cured her child of a developmental type of disorder. This is because many parents want to believe that a simple solution will work. And most parents want to feel that they are in charge of their child's welfare and are doing everything possible to help their child, rather than simply taking orders from a clinician. In other words, bargaining has everything to do with a parent's existing set of beliefs—about themselves, their capabilities, and how the world works.

In their book *The Healing Brain*, neurobiologist Robert Ornstein and physician David Sobel explain the power of belief and its role in all our lives:

> A belief can change the way we see distance, the way we operate, and the way we ready our body for action. What the brain, especially the conscious part, does is first simplify and select information from the outside world . . . Then it decides which system to use and plans actions. At any moment, the content of consciousness is what we are prepared to act on next . . . our view of the world is hardly stable in reality . . . Strong emotions, unexpected or very recent events . . . once in consciousness can have great effects . . . Our changing beliefs shift the mind.[3]

What bread looks like depends on whether you are hungry or not.

—Rumi

When parents in the bargaining phase come up with an alternate solution, they are putting their faith in something that they either want to believe or already believe. Maybe they already believe in health solutions based on diet, hypnosis, or prayer. Those beliefs are likely to influence their choice of treatment for their child's particular challenges. This tendency (which we all have) is called *belief perseverance*: "We tend to pay attention to facts that support our beliefs while we ignore those that contradict our beliefs."[4]

This may help explain why some parents have a difficult time listening to advice from professionals who have devoted much of their lives to research and treatment for specific conditions, and instead will gravitate toward an unproven cure. Of course, some unusual cures *have* been successful, and some traditional doctors have been resistant to promising alternative therapies—which only makes the bargaining phase more confusing. Still, parents may accept medical treatment but want to expand their options.

Alternative Therapies May Satisfy Emotional Needs

In addition to aligning with a parent's existing beliefs, alternative therapies, even when not supported by scientific evidence, sometimes address very pressing emotional needs. The emotional goals of solution seeking for parents may be:

- To be proactive, to take control of decisions that affect my child's care, the overall experience, and the outcomes.
- To participate in my child's care by making my own decisions rather than giving all the power to experts.
- To decrease and manage the fear, stress, and anxiety and to improve my peace of mind.
- To have my child's care providers work with us as a team and show respect for our values, feelings, and choices in all decisions.

- To identify a beneficial treatment outside the domain of doctors, specialists, researchers, and educational specialists, who don't always know everything.

My advice to parents is that it is extremely important to create a team of knowledgeable people to help you make these critical decisions about your child's mental and physical health. This doesn't mean that you can't try something that makes sense to you. It means that you should also take into consideration what other knowledgeable people recommend for your child. Ideally, parents can learn to apply the same rational assessment to what the experts advise and to alternative therapies, taking a truly integrated approach. My rules for this are:

1. Don't endanger your child's health in the excitement over finding a new "guaranteed" treatment that is outside the norm of acceptable treatments.
2. Do be scientific about it. Find out what the research shows. Is there a reputable university or other well-regarded institution behind the research?
3. Ask the expert in charge of this treatment: "How do you know this works? Show me proof." Testimonials from other parents are reassuring but are insufficient means of demonstrating to you that this treatment is effective.
4. Does anyone in the mainstream medical community endorse this treatment? If you see the name of a well-known doctor on a dubious website, find out more. I have seen websites of alternative treatments that bandy names around without exactly securing endorsements.
5. Check out the initials after the names of people who are promoting alternative treatments. I have seen many impressive sounding (read: slick marketing, gullible audience) "doctors" who endorse

products with many initials after their name. Dr. Jones, X.Y.Z., A.A.B.C., may not actually be certified in anything close to what your child's condition is.

> *People don't ask for facts in making up their minds. They would*
> *rather have one good soul-satisfying emotion than a dozen facts.*
> —Robert Keith Leavitt, *Voyages and Discoveries*, 1939

In some cases, special diets, hypnosis, yoga, treatments with the word "neuro" in them, and other alternative treatments have been shown to have a beneficial effect in some children with certain conditions. But when you opt for a particular alternative therapy for your child, make sure not to place an unrealistic amount of confidence in it. Beware of magical thinking—the temptation to think a treatment works based solely on anecdotal evidence and your desire that it be true. Try everything you (reasonably) think might benefit your child, but don't rely on any one alternative method to the exclusion of other treatments. Bargaining for a simpler solution to your child's problem makes sense up to a point, as long as you are not jeopardizing his or her well-being. Later in this chapter, we'll look at some families who tried alternative treatments, and I will share with you some questions to ask practitioners who work with your children.

Meanwhile, it's time to explore the way you, personally, might experience the bargaining phase. There are three types of bargaining patterns I have seen in parents who are still adjusting to their child's diagnosis:

1. The Negotiator—negotiates with the actual diagnosis.
2. The Spiritual Supplicant—externally accepts the diagnosis but internally bargains with self or a "higher power."
3. The Homegrown Scientist—accepts the diagnosis but needs to find his or her own way to work with it.

These approaches reflect the parent's temperament along with his or her existing beliefs. None is right or wrong. The point is that you should be aware of these modes of bargaining and alert to which of them may be influencing your treatment decisions for your child. Let's take a closer look at these three types of bargainers.

The Negotiator

Negotiators are parents who accept that *something* is different about their child but cannot accept the official diagnosis. Why? Because in the bargaining phase, there are still currents of denial and anger swirling beneath the waters. The cognitive system is kicking in to help find solutions, and in order to soothe the emotions, it creates new, more acceptable thoughts about the child's situation. People may draw erroneous conclusions from those thoughts in this stage. Parents, in their strong desire to make meaning of their child's situation, can engage in amped-up thinking that veers away from the practical challenges of a child's disorder.[5] One parent protested, "He's not autistic, he's a genius! We just don't understand his type of genius because we aren't smart enough." Other comments I have heard include:

> "We agree that he has handwriting issues, but it's not a major disorder. Let's just give him a lot of handwriting training."

> "The tutor says that there's no such thing as ADHD and he doesn't believe in testing, so we're just going to stick with the tutor for now."

> "It isn't autism—he's so affectionate with us, he probably has ADHD!"

> "It's true that he gets frustrated, but he can't have an intellectual disability; everyone around him knows he's so bright!"

Some parents refer to their child's condition with a euphemism or incorrect diagnosis because it sounds "better" than the one they received: Dyslexia may be called a dislike of reading. High-functioning autism may be reframed as quirky behavior. Intellectual disability has been referred to as a learning disability. Even medical diagnoses get softened: asthma is "pulmonary irritability." It's not so much denial as it is trying to massage the upsetting information so that it's more palatable.

Selective Listening, Ineffective Treatment

There are, sadly, many examples in my own practice of people who just could not accept their child's diagnosis. The parents of Harrison, a boy with global learning delays, were like this. At age twelve, Harrison could barely read, write, spell, add, or subtract. Harrison was in the seventh grade and reading and writing at a third-grade level. No wonder the boy was utterly demoralized. His parents didn't realize Harrison was delayed because all throughout elementary school, his teachers kindly tended to give him credit for "making progress" and to downplay his actual abilities. They were grading him on effort rather than on accomplishment, so Harrison was getting C's.

Finally, at the end of seventh grade, Harrison's parents went to an open house. They looked at the bulletin boards and the individual desks where the students' work was displayed. When they came to Harrison's desk, they saw to their horror that his story had only three lines, whereas everyone else had written paragraphs. That was when they realized that something was very wrong. They talked to their pediatrician, and she sent the family to me.

Harrison was a sweet boy but very demoralized and frightened to be in my office. The one thing he was enthusiastic about was his video games and television programs. That's really all he would talk about—his favorite games, shows, and TV characters. He had a great imagination, which spun off the characters.

When a child is challenged, I hate to take away anything he or she is passionate about. I think our goal as parents and clinicians is to help the child cultivate passions in life—as many passions as emerge. Because TV and video games were Harrison's passions, I did not recommend taking them away, even though there is a ton of research about the deleterious effects of video games and TV on a child's ability to learn to read (I even wrote my doctoral dissertation on the effects of TV viewing on a child's cognitive development, but this was not the appropriate time to discuss this). My recommendations for Harrison, however, did not include going cold turkey on his TV and video games habit. I recommended a five-day-a-week intensive remediation program for the boy, as well as a number of other things for the parents to do, including cutting back, *very lightly*, on the screen time. A child who is suffering that much in school deserves something pleasurable every day.

Well, Harrison's parents grabbed onto that one point—cutting back on TV—and ignored everything else I recommended. The wife said, "That's it! It's the TV viewing!" And she immediately glared at her husband. Obviously there was already something going on; maybe hubby was a big TV watcher. "We're done! We're getting rid of the TV," she said. And she did it. The husband was willing to go along with his wife's simplistic approach—anything to save the child. Harrison, however, was very upset.

The prohibition against television was the mom's bargaining chip: "I'm willing to do this, and if I do, it *will* be the solution." She didn't do any of the other things I had suggested, for instance, getting an IEP (Individualized Education Plan) from the public school to demonstrate that Harrison was more than two years below grade level, which would have allowed him to get special services. I also suggested that they consider a special education school for Harrison.

In addition, I told them that a twelve-year-old with those problems would benefit from some psychotherapy for a morale boost, or from working with an educational therapist who was good at doing both the remediation and a little therapy.

But Harrison's parents couldn't cope with so many recommendations; they were overwhelmed. The only thing they were able to tackle immediately was shutting off the television. It was their initial bargaining chip, the hope that taking this step would be the magic bullet that would fix Harrison's learning delays. It did not, and Harrison's parents eventually enrolled him in a special school. The person who suffered most because of their bargaining was Harrison, who had to wait even longer to be in an environment where he could learn and succeed.

Bargaining for a Less Serious Diagnosis

Sometimes negotiator-style parents unintentionally place their child at risk by bargaining with the diagnosis itself. Instead of accepting the condition, they substitute a less serious one. Such was the case with Vanessa's parents. Struggling academically and socially, Vanessa started to complain that school was "boring." Her teachers also noticed that she had developed an odd stare; she would gaze off into the distance rather than make eye contact. Vanessa's problems escalated to the point that she was exhibiting severe behavior problems and seemed quite angry. Putting all the pieces together required a neuropsychological exam, so the school referred Vanessa's parents to me. I found that Vanessa had some aspects of high-functioning autism with a number of learning challenges. When I informed her parents, they were adamant that the school not receive my report. Instead they went to their family physician and told him a very different story about Vanessa, emphasizing how "bored" she was, which resulted in a diagnosis of ADHD and a prescription for ADHD medication. With the new diagnosis in hand, they transferred Vanessa to another private school and presented a new set of "facts" about her to the school administration. On paper, the troubling behaviors that the staff at the first school had noticed and which I had verified disappeared. Instead of high-functioning autism and other learning challenges, Vanessa's diagnosis was now ADHD.

Why the switch? Vanessa's parents were willing to handle a diagnosis of ADHD, but not autism, albeit high-functioning autism. At this particular stage in their journey toward accepting their daughter's differences, it was okay to receive a diagnosis, but not *that* diagnosis. Vanessa's parents essentially exchanged one set of facts for another in an attempt to bargain away the more serious condition. It is unclear how Vanessa's adjusted diagnosis and treatment plan will affect her long-term learning capabilities and overall mental well-being. I am sure her parents had their daughter's best interests at heart. It is also likely that their decision-making process involved some intense bargaining—the brain's attempt to make a complex problem seem less complex.

The Spiritual Supplicant

There are no atheists in foxholes, as the saying goes. Many parents find that a crisis with their child opens up a well of spiritual feelings within themselves. As their brains search for solutions, some people become more self-reflective or connect with a spirituality that may have been lying dormant. Prayer is comforting because it is an action people can take; it makes them feel that they are effective agents, that they can create a change. Petitional prayer is a foundational belief in many religions, and there are many testimonials to support prayer as an effective means of support. Prayer and belonging to a spiritual community promote social engagement with others and provide an extra layer of meaning in a world that seems random. To some, prayer is a communication with the ultimate power, inspiring a sense of awe, connectivity, and peaceful presence. Chemically speaking, prayer enhances the brain's soothing neurotransmitters, creating a feeling of well-being. This can also translate into greater feelings of well-being for the child. The downside of spirituality is when parents use prayer or religious practices as a cure, rather than following standard guidelines for helping their child.

Skye was the daughter of such parents. The only child of two artists with deeply rooted spiritual beliefs, her mother and father considered her to be an "old soul," different from average middle-class kids in their neighborhood. She was homeschooled for many years and then placed in an alternative creative school, where the teachers would "best understand her unique talents." Her parents also spent a great deal of time taking her to a variety of religious healers and alternative practitioners around the world in search of something that would improve her overall condition. By age eleven, Skye had already been to Bali in the company of spiritual healers, was on a special diet (gluten-free, dairy-free, and soy-free), and was seeing several specialists weekly, including a dance/movement specialist, art teacher, and a homeopathic healer. Her parents' ideological beliefs prevented her from aligning with standard medical recommendations, year after year.

All these experiences made Skye feel loved and important. She was the center of attention and got to meet many interesting people. But eventually, even the faculty at the alternative school knew that it was time for Skye to be tested using standard methods. The principal asked that Skye receive a neuropsychological evaluation, and that is how I came to meet her.

After evaluating Skye, it was clear that she had an intellectual disability, ADHD, and signs of a genetic disorder. As lovely and well-meaning as her parents' efforts were, if Skye was ever going to be able to function independently, she needed a traditional approach: a medical consultation, an IEP through school, a classroom that met her special needs, medication consultation for ADHD, and social-skills training. Of course, Skye's life would continue to be enriched by the support of her parents. But those alternative efforts would not help her master the basic challenges of day-to-day existence.

The Homegrown Scientist

Some parents accept their child's diagnosis right away, but not the doctors' treatment plan or prognosis. Instead, they roll up their sleeves and vow to solve the problem on their own. They set out on Internet searches, they interview friends and family, and they make multiple appointments with various specialists. They take copious notes. Finding solutions to their child's problems becomes a full-time job.

There is good reason for parents to want to research new or little-known remedies. The final word on many neurodevelopmental disorders has not yet been reached. No one knows what causes autism, or why one child has a learning disability or another child acts funny and quirky. Many developmental conditions that occur secondary to physical disease, prematurity, or birth disorders are poorly understood. There are new genetic findings almost on a daily basis. Science and medicine research fully admit that they don't yet have all the answers to many issues. So researching your child's condition is a worthy endeavor, but it is also a task that may be way beyond the ability of the average parent.

Most parents are not medical researchers or scientists. They must make a living and care for their child, and possibly care for other children and family members too. Yet many parents feel driven to see specialists and comb the Internet until they find the answer . . . *it must be there somewhere* . . . if only they look hard enough. Some parents, as we'll see in the story below, do eventually find an alternate solution on their own. The parents in this case had the resources to keep searching, testing, and reading, and I applaud them for their tenacity and am thrilled with their success. For parents who do not have extraordinary financial resources or scientific knowledge, there is good news: You can hire the services of people who are experts in scouring the medical literature, and they can report to you on the alternative and traditional treatments for your child's condition. More on these medical researchers later in this chapter. First, an inspiring story about one couple who uncovered a largely ignored therapy that changed their child's life.

Healthy Bargaining with a Happy Outcome

Bargaining is about wanting to have a role in your child's treatment plan. The desire to have some control over the treatment often is based on a parent's conclusion that the experts don't know everything. In Jim and Nancy Abrahams's case, they were right. Thanks to their insistence on pursuing every possible lead in order to find a remedy for their son Charlie's condition—and despite the nay-saying of the experts with whom they consulted—the Abrahamses' harrowing story has a healthy outcome.

When Charlie was an infant, he endured multiple daily seizures, often as many as a hundred a day. Every anticonvulsant drug they tried, as well as brain surgery, failed to work. Beside themselves with worry, Nancy and Jim went from neurologist to neurologist searching for something that would help little Charlie overcome this horrific ordeal. One surgeon even suggested a radical procedure called a *corpus callosotomy*—severance of the right brain from the left brain— used as a last resort to treat intractable epilepsy. The Abrahamses were informed that the surgery would not prevent all the seizures, just some. They did not consider this an option.

But the couple tried almost everything else. After eight hospitalizations, numerous CT scans, EEGs, MRIs, and alternative therapies, including homeopathy and faith healing, there was still no remedy for Charlie. Nothing was helping. Finally, while searching through the library, Jim found a book, written in the 1920s, on the ketogenic diet, a special high-fat diet that is used for difficult-to-treat seizures. There were many other studies documenting the diet's efficacy, including one published by Johns Hopkins in 1992, just a year before Charlie got sick, documenting fifty-eight consecutive children with drug resistant epilepsy in which 29 percent became seizure-free and another 30 percent were significantly improved using a ketogenic diet. Although rigorous adherence to the diet is required in order for it to be effective, Jim and Nancy figured it was definitely worth a try, and under the direction of staff at Johns Hopkins University, they started Charlie on the diet.

Interestingly, the Abrahamses met with resistance from the five pediatric neurologists with whom they had consulted. One neurologist told them, "Yes, I know about this diet, but it may not work, and it's very hard to maintain." Jim and Nancy's response was, "Where in medical school do they teach what would be too hard for the family of a critically ill child to endure?" So they put Charlie on the diet and within a few weeks the seizures had ceased and he was able to go off all medications. Charlie was on the diet for about five years, and after that he no longer needed it. He is now in his twenties and seizure-free.

The website for the Charlie Foundation (which the Abrahamses founded to help other parents of children with seizures) points out that the ketogenic diet does not always work miracles, as it did for Charlie. A randomized controlled study documenting the ketogenic diet's efficacy was published in 2008.[6] Additionally, studies that have followed children on the diet for long periods reveal that one-third of children treated with the ketogenic diet have greater than 90 percent seizure control, with half of these children becoming seizure-free. An additional one-third experience a 50 percent reduction in seizures. The remaining one-third discontinue the diet due to its ineffectiveness or its difficulty.[7]

When I spoke with Nancy Abrahams, she told me that a key lesson she learned during Charlie's ordeal is that it is crucial for parents to be their own advocates. Remembering the time of Charlie's severe difficulties, she said, "There's nothing more lonely than being the parent of a disabled child in the park." She said one reason for taking charge of your child's health issue is that otherwise you become a hostage to the label. Nancy feels that healthy bargaining is a refusal to bow down to the label and instead to insist: "I am going to find something beyond what the experts are recommending—something that will truly help my child." Nancy believes that, on the one hand, when you surrender to your child's diagnosis, you're relieved because you know what's wrong and you know what to do. But on the other hand, you may be unwilling to surrender to the recommended treatment.

Receiving a difficult diagnosis for your child can disempower you as a parent. One minute you are in charge of raising your beautiful child, and the next, you get a diagnosis that completely takes over, relaying the message: *You are not in charge; the experts are in charge. Here's what's wrong with your kid, and here's what you have to do.*

Parents like the Abrahamses who engage in bargaining by becoming well informed and proactive in overseeing their child's treatment feel empowered. As Jim Abrahams states, "We have taken control of so many lesser issues in our family—meals, bedtimes, TV hours. Why not have that same attitude with the most important issue in our families: our children's health? In the worst case we have learned something new; in the best case, we have improved either our lives or the lives of our children. There is no downside."

Jim is a film producer, and he produced a made-for-TV movie in 1997 titled *First Do No Harm*, starring Meryl Streep. Inspired by the Abrahamses' experiences with Charlie, the film has been described as "a true story of one woman's struggles against a narrow-minded medical establishment."

The Abrahamses did their research *and* they included the professionals: Charlie's dietary regimen, while originally initiated by his parents, was overseen by nutritional experts at a reputable medical institution. An important moral to this story is that if you uncover a plausible treatment option, be sure to enlist the approval of your doctor before attempting anything on your own.

What's Out There? Help with Treatment Research

There are two factors that make it difficult for many parents to research their child's condition the way the Abrahamses did: time and expertise. Most people do not have the time to conduct an intensive level of research, and even if they did, they would not understand what they were reading. For the majority of childhood developmental variations, there is no need to reinvent the wheel—a robust selection of research-based standard-of-care treatments already exists, and your therapist or doctor will recommend them. However, if you are the type of parent who needs to make sure you have turned over every stone, or you are convinced that your child's condition is unusual and is not being addressed appropriately, there are places you can turn for help.

One option is to hire a medical researcher to investigate the available treatments and explain them to you. Medical researchers may be practicing psychiatrists and psychologists, researchers, or scientists. They will charge a fee to research the existing medical literature (meaning studies appearing in traditional medical journals and other mainstream academic sources, or any other area you would like them to investigate). The cost depends on how much has been written about the particular condition and on the price of medical journals that charge for access to articles. If you are in touch with other parents whose children have the same condition, you could pool your resources to pay for the researcher. The services researchers provide include but are not limited to:

- Finding and reviewing free medical abstracts and articles from sources such as PubMed.
- Finding and reviewing abstracts and articles that can be accessed with a fee.
- Helping parents develop search terms for PubMed, and after they have done the initial search, reading the abstracts for them and helping them sort through conflicting evidence.
- Culling relevant information from the What Works Clearinghouse, an organization that reviews the research on different programs, products, practices, and policies in education.
- Conducting searches for rare conditions and conditions where medical and psychiatric symptoms overlap.

If you have attempted to do any research on your child's condition yourself, you already know how difficult it can be to interpret the medical jargon or understand the implications of the statistics. It may be very empowering to have that research conducted by someone who knows how to do it, can explain it to you, and also is objective.

But please remember to not get too caught up in the "seeking" of alternatives, remember that your team has already done so much research for your child already. Seeking can have an addictive quality; you may not know when to stop, when enough is enough.

Finding out about the most effective treatments is only one part of the research process. How do you know which of those treatments is available through the school system or other social services? For relatively little expense (in light of the information you will get), you can hire an educational advocate to help you navigate the system. The Individuals with Disabilities Education Act (IDEA) is a nationwide law that ensures services to children with disabilities, but it's a bureaucracy with confusing acronyms and a complex website. It certainly helps to have someone walk you through it and pinpoint every service to which your child is entitled. Dona Wright, the mother of a boy with autism, became an educational advocate after struggling to get the right services for her son. You'll learn more about Dona in Chapter 6.

Many parents gain a sense of solace and control from researching their child's condition, but for others, it is a tremendous burden to feel as if they must personally uncover every potential treatment hidden in every last corner of the Internet. If that is the case for you, I encourage you to take advantage of reputable options for research.

> **Hope for a miracle but always have a Plan B (the recommended plan) in your pocket.**

My word of advice: Hope for a miracle but always have a Plan B (the recommended plan) in your pocket. You may be losing valuable time for standard remediation if you ignore the experts and embark on a lengthy search for alternatives. All children deserve early identification and early treatment. A young child's brain is very plastic, meaning it is malleable and easily absorbs new information. You don't want your child to miss critical windows of learning opportunity.

Healthy Skepticism

In this chapter, we have seen that some parents of children with differences bargain in order to receive a lesser diagnosis. Others engage in bargaining to find a less daunting treatment than the one recommended by their child's teacher, pediatrician, or psychologist. Often parents bargain to find answers on their own because they simply don't trust the professionals. And sometimes skepticism concerning the "experts" is highly warranted. I can sympathize with many of the parental protests I hear. For example:

> "My child's school didn't test him early enough."

> "The educational specialist didn't offer a complete enough treatment plan."

> "We got bad advice from our pediatrician, who didn't think there was anything wrong with our child."

> "Our doctor doesn't seem very knowledgeable about learning differences."

> "The psychiatrist we consulted only wanted to prescribe meds—nothing more."

> "Our pediatrician prescribed too many meds, without sufficiently warning us of side effects."

> "The professionals we consulted were completely disinterested in alternative treatments and derided us for even considering anything outside the mainstream."

These are very legitimate concerns, especially given that children develop at different rates and respond differently to a variety of treatments. Not all treatments work for all children and sometimes what works initially stops working and new treatments need to be added. Unlike medical diagnoses that definitively affirm you have cancer or diabetes, with neurodevelopmental disorders we work in gray areas. Despite the use of functional MRIs and PET scans, or neuropsychological tests that attempt to pinpoint a diagnosis, most people in the field will readily admit that these can be imprecise. Even when we professionals are doing our jobs superbly, often there is no definitive diagnosis for a child's condition. And when teachers, doctors, educational specialists, psychologists, and others don't take the time to help parents understand the particulars of their child's situation, or are not sympathetic to the fact that parents need to be guided as to how to most effectively help their child, there is good reason to become frustrated or skeptical. So I understand when a parent resists a particular diagnosis or proceeding with a professional's recommended remediations. And I respect a parent's need to learn as much as they can before settling on their preferred method of treatment.

My bottom line: I strongly believe in empowering parents to make the final decisions for their children. I feel most comfortable if these decisions are rooted in scientific empirical data and advice from trusted professionals, but I acknowledge that sometimes alternate therapies that have little or no scientific studies backing them have helped some families. But I also know that there are a great many unproven, nonscientific, and essentially worthless treatments out there, so you have to be very careful about trying these methods. Time is usually a big consideration for your child. A year spent on an alternate therapy that does not work is no small thing. Your child's self-esteem may decrease; your child may even blame him- or herself for the therapy not working. Meanwhile, the learning or developmental difficulties persist or get worse. When the alternative treatment you may have settled on during the bargaining phase fails to yield positive results in your child's condition, you may be left with Internet-search burnout, wasted dollars on ineffective nutritional supplements or phony treatments, exhaustion, and hopelessness— which can lead to depression and isolation, the subject of our next chapter.

Bargaining Guidelines

Please remember that as a parent, you are emotionally vulnerable when it comes to your child. Bargaining is a particularly vulnerable stage because you are using your prefrontal cortex to seek solutions but are still emotionally overstimulated because your child's well-being is at stake. Here are some guidelines that I hope will help ground you in reasonable seeking and lead toward more emotional acceptance:

1. Well-meaning friends and family may offer you alternative treatments that may differ from the standard of care that has been recommended. Investigate the alternatives if you want, but do a lot of research and consult with your professional before making a decision.

2. If you have given an alternative treatment time to be effective and it is clearly not working, don't waste more time on it. Consult with a reputable professional to consider the next step.

3. Read about the latest breakthrough treatment or the memoir by a celebrity parent whose child has what your child has—but don't take any one person's word for what works. Do your research. What do respected journals, organizations, universities, and hospitals have to say on the subject?

4. Be skeptical of a treatment that claims to cure everything from dyslexia to ADHD to bipolar disorder to low self-esteem. As far as I know, there is no one remedy for multiple learning and mood disorders.

5. Learn to spot phony research claims on the Internet, TV, and in the print media. Who is backing up these claims? What reputable sources stand behind these claims? What is the actual evidence that the treatment really works?

6. Acknowledge that you may be in the bargaining stage and that your decisions may not be purely rational. At the same time, acknowledge that you are doing the best you can to ensure your child's well-being.

7. Find a team of professionals whom you can trust. In many cases the people who claim to be experts have limited experience and a lot to gain monetarily from enlisting your confidence. Don't

mistake salesmanship for expertise. When in doubt, ask your primary physician for guidance.

8. Your religious community can be a valuable source of comfort and support. There is nothing wrong with feeling more spiritual or discovering the healing power of the divine. By all means, include faith-based activities in your family structure. But don't ignore other therapies.

CHAPTER FIVE

The Depression Trap

*We've consulted with so many specialists. We've tried social skills
classes, dietary modifications, different therapies and medications
and educational remediations. Some things didn't work; some therapies work but are so hard to keep up. After almost a year of this, I
am burnt out. With all our efforts and struggles, sometimes it just
feels like too much for me.*

—Diana, mother of nine-year-old Gaby, diagnosed with ADHD,
reading disorder, and seizure disorder

• • •

At some point along the journey of caring for your special child,
feelings of depression are to be expected. Please take heart in
the fact that you are not alone. Depression is a universal and deeply
human emotion. While some parents may have experienced depressive feelings even before having a child, those feelings can become
more pronounced in this particular phase of your journey. After the
energy spent in denial and anger, in pro-
tecting the image of your ideal child, **You are
not alone.**
through the phase of looking for answers
and seeking solutions, negotiating treat-
ments and exploring different therapies, you might start feeling like
you're running on empty. Despite all the surges of optimism, all the
improvements or hope for improvements, there will be times when

you hit bottom. Yet depression too can be seen as a phase you can pass through. I want to validate your feelings, and I hope to guide you through this specific type of situational depression and help you move forward to a better place.

As a parent caring for a child with special needs, it can be very hard to admit to depression. You may not even think you're depressed. Maybe you're too busy chauffeuring your child to all his or her appointments and keeping up with your other obligations to consider your own emotions. Or maybe you're not the type to feel sorry for yourself. *I'm fine*, you may think, even though there is the nagging sense that you're not quite yourself. If you fall into the "I'm fine" camp, I encourage you to pay close attention to this chapter anyway. I strongly suspect you will find it relevant.

> **Depression too can be seen as a phase you can pass through.**

Diana, the mom in the opening quote, had a series of typical and understandable reactions to the unfamiliar and demanding situation she found herself in: raising a daughter with multiple disorders. After a year of nonstop efforts, the chronic stress was taking its toll. Diana told me that in addition to feeling that her daily routine had become too much for her, she felt totally isolated from her friends. She couldn't join in their conversations about how to improve their kids' grade from a B to an A, or which camp had the best sports program. Diana's daughter Gaby still could not read, dress herself, or hold a pencil. And Gaby's seizures prevented her from going to sleepaway camp or ever being unsupervised. As a single mother, Diana did not have the support of a mate. "I feel like I'm in no-man's-land," she said. "I don't want to make this all about me, but I'm feeling so down, and I know that's not doing Gaby any good. I'm so ashamed that I can't handle all of this myself. After all, I volunteered to be a single mom."

Diana had tried going to psychotherapy to talk about her problems and her uneven moods, but she did not find it helpful. The psychotherapist seemed to focus on the biochemical aspects of her symptoms rather than addressing her overall situation, which included the chronic stress of having a special-needs child, her lack of access to social support, and her grief over the loss of an idealized child. The psychotherapist apparently did not take into account how Diana's life had changed since Gaby's diagnosis. The "real" Diana, BD (before diagnosis), was vibrant, energetic, and optimistic. When Diana thought about the woman she used to be compared to the way she felt now, her mood sank even lower. This young mother was going through a depression specifically related to the stresses of parenting an atypical child. Recognizing and addressing this type of situational depression requires more than a label and a pill, although antidepressants can be very helpful. (The discussion in this chapter about situational depression is not intended to promote or disparage the use of prescribed medication for depression.)

After the rush of feelings when a child's diagnosis is given, after the denial has subsided, the anger has worn itself out, and a parent has researched all the available treatments, the reality can no longer be avoided: *My child is unique but also different, difficult, unusual, or disabled. He or she is not going to have an easier life by a wave of my magic wand. This is a condition that my child and I will have to struggle with. I can't see a light at the end of the tunnel, and it makes me feel very defeated.* Yet even to think those thoughts may cause tremendous feelings of guilt.

If you admit to being depressed about your child's condition, you may feel that you are coming up short in your role as a strong, nurturing parent. When a thought such as *I can't do this anymore* creeps in, you may feel ashamed that your love for your child has not given you superhuman powers. You may also feel guilty for letting your child's diagnosis get you down when there are other children out there with more serious problems. Since many atypical children often look like "garden variety" kids (at least in some situations), you may instantly feel sad and guilty when a stranger in the supermarket compliments you on your adorable child. Maybe you berate yourself: *Why can't I simply appreciate my precious child? Why am I so down all the time?*

There are perfectly valid reasons for your despondency. What the stranger in the market doesn't know is that when your adorable child comes home, he may throw himself on the floor in fits of rage because he is on sensory overload. Or perhaps your little girl becomes terribly anxious every day before school, and there's little you can do to calm her. Or your son spends most of the day bouncing up and down as his erratic moods shift. It is completely understandable that you will feel waves of despair during your attempts to successfully navigate the atypical parenting path that has been handed to you.

A Normal Response to an Extraordinary Challenge

Depression is often seen as a medical diagnosis caused by a chemical change inside your body. But depression can also be a reaction, one in a series of several emotional reactions that we are discussing in this book. Grieving the loss of your original expectations and seeing your beloved child struggle can cause depression (just as any loss can). Our brains are wired with a natural capacity for resilience, but there are times when you can lose your ability to be flexible and joyful. Instead, you may become flat, emotionally reactive or under-reactive, and feel defeated in battle. It's normal to sometimes cave in—to the reality of the diagnosis, the reality of your child's multiple needs, and the reality of the extra burden you will have to carry for an indefinite amount of time.

As debilitating and "wrong" as depression may sometimes feel, it is actually within the normal range of parenting's emotional spectrum. Temporary depression is a mood state that may accompany parenthood from the very beginning. By the third day after giving birth, many postpartum moms experience some level of depression. This is due to hormonal surges, even when your brain tells you it is abnormal to feel so blue when you finally have that lovely baby in your arms. Unfortunately, postpartum depression is not something you can reason yourself out of. Instead, you must wait for your body to recover from childbirth and move toward homeostasis—biological and emotional equilibrium.

A resilient brain/body system works to achieve homeostasis in multiple ways, continually regulating things such as temperature, breathing, hormones, neurotransmitters, and emotions. That is why most postpartum mothers eventually return to their normal state of mind. And most of the time, when your emotions as a parent get out of whack, you will soon naturally self-regulate and recover your sense of balance and perspective. That is, unless the stress is unrelenting, the condition seems so disheartening, and the support and solutions seem so remote.

Parents Can Feel Helpless

Parenting any child, typical or atypical, can make you feel as if you've lost control of your life. Every new parent must go through a period of adjustment, and for many, it's a wrenching transition. But although most parents occasionally become depressed while raising their kids, depression among parents of children with disabilities is especially crushing. It's important to know, however, that feeling depressed for short periods of time does not necessarily mean you have clinical depression. (See the box on page 164 for a description of that condition.) Even without a previous diagnosis of depression in your life, you can be feeling low for one or more of the following reasons:

- It is very difficult to see your child suffer.
- It is very difficult to realize that your child is so different from the others.
- It is very difficult to watch your child's self-esteem get battered.
- It is very difficult to be responsible for your atypical child's needs and to have little time or energy left for yourself, your partner, your other children, or your friends.
- In cases where a diagnosis is elusive or there are multiple diagnoses, it is very difficult not to know exactly what is wrong with your child, or what to do about it.
- Fear and anxiety about the well-being and future of your child can sometimes overpower your best defenses.
- You are plain worn out, worried about the future, and feelings of defeat can sometimes overwhelm you.
- Your family dynamics are altered; you may worry that you will ignore your other children by focusing on your special-needs child.
- You may fear, deep down, that you are simply not up to the stresses and challenges of raising a special-needs child.
- You may not be able to afford the best treatment for your child.
- The relationship with your spouse may be suffering because you have different ideas about how to deal with your child's problem.
- Since some developmental disorders may be largely invisible, you may wonder if you are crazy for being so stressed.
- Having a child with a similar condition that you had as a child can uncover many uncomfortable feelings that you thought were long forgotten. Since many conditions have a genetic component, this is more common than you might think.

Later in this chapter, we'll explore how depressive feelings can sometimes serve a positive purpose, increasing your compassion and empathy. But no one wants to be depressed, and these emotions can become debilitating. To work yourself through the depression stage, you need to understand its neuropsychological roots. With that knowledge, you can develop a strategy that will carry you past depression and on to the more peaceful and productive acceptance phase.

The Neuropsychology of Depression

Depression is the common cold of the mental health world. More than 15 percent of the population in the United States will have a depressive episode at some point, with women twice as vulnerable as men. It is estimated that 11 percent of the population is taking antidepressants; for women, that figure is 20 percent, or one in five. Clearly, people live complex lives and depressive feelings are common. Yet researchers have found that many who are prescribed antidepressants may not actually be clinically depressed (see box on page 164). They are having a depressed reaction in response to a specific trauma or situation. In time, many people will return to their "normal selves," adjust to their circumstances, stop taking medications, and say good-bye to their therapists.

There is no simple explanation for what causes some people to become stuck in depression and spiral downward into major depression, while others are more successful in bouncing back. We do know that a combination of genetic predisposition, the quality of your original parent-child relationship (known as "attachment"), and the level of current and ongoing stressors are important predictors of whether your depressed feelings are going to be episodic or recurrent and chronic. In addition, being connected with a community of friends or supportive family versus feeling alone can contribute to a person's level of depression.

You may feel listless when you are depressed, but your brain is quite active. In fact, there is a war raging in there. In Chapter 3, "Anger and Blame," we talked about how the amygdala (the emotional

---

DEFINITION: CLINICAL DEPRESSION

Clinical depression is the more severe form of depression, also known as major depression or major depressive disorder. It includes symptoms such as depressed mood, loss of interest in pleasurable activities, significant weight loss or weight gain, insomnia or hypersomnia, sluggish behavior, difficulty making decisions. It can also include suicidal ideation. Major depression is not the same as depressive feelings that are caused by a loss, bereavement, or a medical issue.

---

brain) "hijacks" the neocortex (thinking part of the brain). The amygdala is also highly activated when you're depressed, preventing the neocortex from finding logical solutions to stressful events. The hippocampus is one of the important memory areas of the brain. Research has found that the hippocampus shrinks in the brain of a depressed person, which may explain the fogginess and forgetfulness of people who are depressed.

When you are depressed, your neocortex (the thinking brain) attempts to reasonably assess stressful or unpleasant situations, but it is stuck like a needle on a vinyl LP—it keeps replaying a litany of your predicament in a ruminating way. Depression is the combination of dark thoughts and sad feelings that occurs when the thinking brain (neocortex) and the feeling brain (amygdala/limbic system) get caught in a back and forth dance: Rumination and brooding reinforce that dark sadness. While this is the mind's attempt to resolve the problem behind the sadness, it actually does little to help and keeps you stuck in the rut. If you could create a chart illustrating this replay loop, it would look like this:

Depression is usually accompanied by physiological changes such as insomnia and loss of appetite or overeating. Your mental and physical state during the depression phase is the flip side of the denial phase: Instead of feeling frozen and on automatic pilot, you experi-

RATIONAL THOUGHT	EMOTIONS	MEMORY
I need to get up this morning.	I'm overwhelmed; what's the point?	Why did I set the alarm?
I have to stop this child's tantrum!	I can't, I'm exhausted.	Why is he screaming? I can't follow this.
I must be strong for my child, or at least fake it.	I can't fake it, I'm too sad.	I can't remember why I need to be strong.

ence your feelings all too strongly. Stress hormones such as cortisol are elevated, and normal biological processes such as libido, appetite, sleep patterns, and general levels of energy are suppressed.

The Brain's Negativity Bias and "ANTs"

There is another element in the neuropsychology of the brain that adds to the potential for depression: It is the human condition to see things in a negative light. This is due to the brain being wired as an anticipation machine for survival, scouting out danger and modulating possible fear. When we are not aware of the brain's negativity bias, we may perceive life as a series of defeats, challenges, and burdens. However, we can and we must cultivate our mind to work through this bias and past it. Research has found

Become aware of your ANTs: automatic negative thoughts.

that people with difficult lives are not necessarily more depressed than people with easy lives; the determining factor is often their personal level of resilience and how they react to stress.

How do you turn a potential for negative cycling and emotional disaster into resilience? How do you rescue yourself and teach your brain to respond neutrally or positively? Later in this chapter, I will give you a toolbox of proven techniques to get you out of this emotional quagmire. But for now, I want you to become aware of your ANTs: automatic negative thoughts. The field of cognitive behavioral psychology holds that the way we think about things has a big impact on the way we feel. When we allow our negative thoughts to overrule our thinking brain, it affects our emotional brain. Let's identify some common ANTs:

1. **"Always" and "never."** Do these words crowd your thinking, "Sheesh, why does she *always* have to throw a tantrum?" Or "I *never* get a break in my life!" These are overgeneralizations that can lead you into a spiral of all-or-nothing thinking. For now, simply notice when you are doing it. If you can smile when you hear yourself say it, you are on your way to a better outlook.

   > **Noticing is learning.**

2. **"It's all my fault."** Taking blame for your child's condition or the situation that you have found yourself in is a common self-blame game that parents can get sucked into. You may turn your frustration inward, thinking, "I caused this," or "I am not strong enough for this challenge." Again, noticing is learning. When you are aware of the negative self-talk, you can teach yourself to change it.

3. **Catastrophizing.** It's the familiar 3:00 a.m. litany: *How will he grow up? Will she be able to live independently? How will he support himself?* These are important questions, but catastrophic ruminating at 3:00 a.m. does not serve you well. Stay in the moment and learn to focus on the here and now. Take life one step at a

time. Slow your mind down. Nothing is as bad as it looks in the dark of the night.

You don't have to control your thoughts. You just have to stop letting them control you.

—Dan Millman, author and lecturer

Emotional Quicksand: When Your Worry Brain Doesn't Shut Off

Humans are not the only creatures who experience depression. Other mammals can become depressed when they feel socially rejected, defeated, or threatened. They can also be very protective of their offspring and grieve when they lose a young one. But while other animals can grieve a loss, humans are the only species that grieves *abstract loss.* Losing your best friend or a death in the family are tangible losses— an absence from your life. Having a child with a diagnosis is an abstract loss. Your child exists, but you still mourn the loss of the ideal child you thought you would parent. And what causes you to keep returning to that abstract loss? Your uniquely human ability to ruminate on what might have been and worry about what is yet to come.

The human brain's frontal cortex is continually reflecting on the past and planning for the future. When it is stymied or defeated, it begins to imagine the worst outcome and plan for hardship. From an evolutionary perspective, this makes a lot of sense. It enabled our ancient ancestors to survive in the savannahs, and it helps us prepare for upcoming events such as a college exam or a job interview. Afterward, we may review the event in our mind: *Did I pass? Did I say the right things? Am I going to succeed?* In this way, our brain is constantly on the alert, protecting from incoming danger and assessing the threat after it has passed.

But in cases of chronic stress, planning and reflecting may not result in a solution that seems achievable, so it morphs into worry and remorse: *Why didn't I ask the doctor all the questions I had planned? What could I have done differently when Susie froze up and wouldn't board the bus? How will she ever manage without me? Is she going to make it to college? Will she ever be in a relationship? Will the tantrums ever end? How can I keep this up forever? Is she going to get worse?* And onward into a negative cycle that leaves you exhausted and hopeless. But you can learn how to stop your worry brain from generating those exhausting negative thoughts. A technique called "Thought Stopping" is easy to learn and can alleviate anxiety or mild depression. Focus on a negative thought and say aloud "Stop!" Hearing your own voice can strengthen your commitment to stop it. As you practice this technique, you will be able to exercise more control over your runaway catastrophic thinking. If you want to learn more about this approach from a professional, look for a therapist who is trained in cognitive behavioral therapy (CBT). Learning to control your own mind can be a gateway to enhanced personal efficacy and feelings of well-being.

Know When to Seek Professional Help

It is common for parents who have no prior history of depression to become despondent due to the stress of caring for an atypical child. In parents who do have a history of depression, the situation can become more complicated. Your previous experiences, genetic makeup, and emotional disorders influence how you will navigate the journey toward acceptance of your child. Some of my clients were diagnosed with chronic depression long before receiving their child's diagnosis. Some have been in treatment for depression—in therapy or taking antidepressants or both—for years. The added stress of overseeing their child's condition and treatment may worsen their depression.

Sometimes, when a person has been living with low-grade but pervasive depression, having an atypical child can send him or her into major depression. If you think this could be happening to you, realize that it can be an opportunity for you to get the help you need and deserve. There is no shame in asking for help as a parent. Medication, individual therapy, or a support group may be the catalyst that improves your mood and outlook, as well as enabling you to keep functioning for your family. If you have a history of depression or feel unable to carry out your daily activities, it is critical that you consult with a psychiatrist, as medications for depression can be effective. However, a psychiatrist may not understand that what you are going through is part of the process of learning to accept your atypical child, and you should feel free to explain that to him or her. Your child's condition has resulted in significant changes for you and your family, and adapting to those changes isn't easy. So get the help you need, and do everything you can to feel okay. There is deep wisdom in the ability to surrender and say, "I need help." So please go for it.

> **There is no shame in asking for help as a parent.**

> *Have patience with all things, but chiefly have patience with yourself. Do not lose courage in considering your own imperfections but instantly set about remedying them—every day begin the task anew.*
>
> —Saint Francis de Sales

Types of Treatments

There are many types of popular psychotherapy techniques available, but let's take a look at the two prominent therapies currently being practiced: cognitive behavioral therapy (CBT) and interpersonal or psychodynamic therapy. CBT focuses on teaching you how to reframe your thoughts more positively. Research has shown that CBT can be highly effective in treating depression. It targets the cortex (the thinking brain), reshaping how you process information. CBT trains the brain to use different thinking circuits, to switch off ruminative modes of thinking, and to practice relating differently to negative thoughts and feelings. CBT holds that negative thinking leads to depression, and that the way out of it is to "change the thoughts, change the feelings."

One good aspect of CBT is that it typically lasts for a brief period of time and is targeted for results. There are many CBT-trained therapists. To locate those in your area, you can try the websites Good Therapy.org and BeckInstitute.org, but there are many others. You can also ask your primary physician for a referral.

Interpersonal or psychodynamic therapy, sometimes called *the talking cure*, focuses more on the underlying reasons for depression. This is considered the more traditional type of therapy in that your therapist will ask you about your childhood, the quality of your relationships, and your patterns of coping in your life. Along with building insight about yourself, you might experience catharsis (relief) from just talking about your situation. Some therapists will be able to combine both types of therapies.

In addition to the insights and coping strategies you learn in therapy, the personal relationship that develops between client and therapist can be very helpful. Both types of therapy have been shown to be as effective as medication in many cases of depression. But there is no shame in taking medication; what matters is that you find a way to feel stronger and more positive, and to function better in your daily life.

I am bigger than this.

I am not my struggles.

I will survive this and overcome it.

I will keep moving forward.

Nothing will keep me down.

I will rebuild myself stronger than before.
Watch me.

—Author Unknown

The Western View of Depression

In part because we now know so much about neurobiology, and in part because the field of mental health was founded on a medical model, most Western mental health professionals view depression as an illness. A medical model is, by definition, symptom-based. Treat the symptoms and reduce or eliminate them—that constitutes a cure. Your despondency and emotional flatness (with a strong wish to curl up in bed) is considered a disease that needs to be treated. And anyone who has experienced true major depression can attest to the fact that it is debilitating and serious.

Although depression is known to be a complex condition, situational depression in parents who are struggling with the multiple needs of their atypical child is not always viewed as a significant event among those the medical community who treat adult mood disorders. Parents are usually sized up as adults with depression rather than "parent overwhelmed with atypical kid depression," especially among clinicians who are trained to look for symptoms rather than situations. But your depression as a parent, your feelings of being overwhelmed, your isolation, and your sadness are directly related to issues with your child. It's a type of situational depression that has yet to be adequately acknowledged. A similar lack of understanding used to accompany symptoms of post-traumatic stress disorder (PTSD). Bessel van der Kolk, a pioneer in the field of post-traumatic stress, states:

> The development of post-traumatic stress disorder (PSTD) as a diagnosis has created an organized framework for understanding

how people's biology, conceptions of the world, and personalities are inextricably intertwined and shaped by experience. The PTSD diagnosis has reintroduced the notion that many "neurotic" symptoms are not the results of some mysterious . . . genetically based irrationality, but of people's inability to come to terms with real experiences that have overwhelmed their capacity to cope. In important ways, an experience does not really exist until it can be named.[1]

In other words, you are in a special category of persons that has not yet been named, but does indeed exist. We can only hope that current and new research will lead to further clarification in the medical world, and that parents of special-needs children will get the validation and consideration they deserve.

Meanwhile, conventional treatment of depression in adults tends to involve a combination of medication and psychotherapy, with a greater emphasis on medication, especially if one consults with a psychiatrist. While medications such as SSRIs (Zoloft and Paxil, among many others) and the newer SNRIs (such as Cymbalta) help many people, research has found that nearly 50 percent of patients do not get long-term relief from antidepressants. For those patients, other means of treatment are necessary. Some studies have found that individual psychotherapy is equally successful in the short term as antidepressants and more effective in the long run. In addition, many people are ashamed to admit they need medication to treat their depression. Perhaps they shouldn't feel that way, but they do, and it may keep them from seeking help at all.

Prescribing Pills While Missing the Obvious

The experience of Susan, a thirty-eight-year-old mother of three, is not as uncommon as you might think. Susan's oldest, Jane, had been diagnosed with ADHD, hyperactive-impulsive type, at age twelve.

Her second child, Ashley, was eight and had recently been diagnosed with dyslexia and ADHD, inattentive type. Her youngest, three-year-old Austin, was an undiagnosed handful. Increasingly unable to cope, Susan went to see a psychiatrist. She had begun to drink alcohol every night as a way to release the tension, and she hoped the psychiatrist could give her some tools for handling her demanding life. While writing a prescription for antidepressant medication, the psychiatrist casually mentioned that Susan might like to take a vacation with the children. "It could be a nice way to feel closer to them and to get to know them better," he counseled.

Susan stared at him, dumbfounded. It was as if the doctor assumed that her depression was not linked to the stress of her children's needs but simply a coincidence. Her mind raced with angry questions: Did he think she was depressed because of a random chemical imbalance and taking a vacation with her children would help? How did he not realize that having three children with serious behavioral and learning diagnoses was draining the daylights out of her? Susan did not return to this particular doctor, nor did she fill her prescription. She did, however, arrange a four-day visit to her sister, who lived out of state. Her husband and a babysitter watched the kids while she was gone. Being with her sister, getting some down time, pampering herself, and most of all having long, nourishing conversations—adult conversations—with someone who understood and supported her was the best medication for Susan. While it did not solve her problems, the relief it provided made her realize that she needed similar support and respite from caretaking on a regular basis at home.

An Alternative Way to Think About Your Depression

There are ways other than medication and symptom reduction therapy to approach the situational depression of a parent. It begins with recognizing that feeling depressed is a normal response to stress. In his book *Saving Normal*, Allen Frances writes:

> Homeostasis and time are great natural healers and most people can resiliently right themselves and regain their normal balance . . . Prematurely resorting to medication short circuits the traditional pathways of restorative natural healing: support from family, friends, community, making needed life changes, offloading excessive stress, pursuing hobbies and interests, exercise, rest, distraction, a change of pace.[2]

Alternative and complementary medicine does not work from the disease model. Instead, you can view depression as being out of balance, separated from your life force. This alternative view (which is thought to be rooted in Eastern philosophy, particularly Buddhism) holds that the overreaction of your mind to stresses, both real and imagined, drains your energy and causes the separation. The unremitting stress of parenting a special child, even after you recover from the shock, can leave even the strongest of parents emotionally wiped out, with their last watt of energy focused on their child. In that place of constant vigilance, it's very easy to forget who you are as an individual, or that you ever were a person other than "Lucie's mom." This separation from your self—from your life force—can be a very real cause of depression. From an Eastern holistic model, you have lost perspective and lost your connection to yourself.

It's important to consider if there are specific reasons you are unhappy, apart from just identifying your symptoms, because symptoms are only part of the picture. If you find yourself overreacting to the stress of raising your child or children, seeing yourself as abnormal or ill is not an effective way to work through your emotions. At the same time, depression is a sign that something needs to change. In Chapter 6, you will read about some parents who were able to shift their lives in positive ways despite living in very difficult situations. Taking care of lower level feelings of depression can help avert the possibility of major depression later, new studies suggest. This pre-emptive approach includes some self-help techniques and psychotherapy.

Are You Depressed or Oppressed?
The Perils of Over-Involvement

For at least fifty years, attachment theory has been a core concept of human psychology. Developed by John Bowlby, attachment theory holds that the quality of the bond between parent and child determines the future mental health of the child. The child learns that the parent is dependable, and thus the child becomes "securely attached." Less optimal attachment states are "avoidant," "ambivalent," or "disorganized" patterns of attachment, which are reflective of the suboptimal interactions that can be disconnecting, inconsistent, or terrifying and neglectful while the child was very young.

Attachment theory is a bedrock concept of child development, and yet for atypical children, the expected patterns of interaction of secure attachment may not look at all like what one expects. All atypical children need to feel safe and securely attached as much as typical children, yet they may behave differently or act more rejecting of parents' attempts to create a safe and secure relationship. While all children are wired to respond to their parents' love and attention, atypical children may respond quite differently; it may not be due to "avoidant" or "ambivalent" attachment patterns but rather how their social interaction circuits are wired. Seeking secure attachment and social-emotional interactive behaviors depends on two different brain pathways that can develop independently of one another. A neuro-atypical child might act socially quite unusual or even rejecting, while simultaneously retaining a strong inner need for attachment. Parents must learn different ways to interpret their child's atypical signals, which is challenging enough in itself. Moreover, while early attachment patterns will leave a solid imprint on a child's mental well-being, it is certainly not the only factor that affects a child's socio-emotional development. Genetics, natural temperament, and environment are a few of the other important influences. Variations in neural development are not due to attachment experiences, even though they may shape how attachment needs are conveyed by the child through atypical social interactions.

Developing bonds of reciprocity between parent and child, and interactions that are supposed to yield securely attached children, do not necessarily work the same way in children who are developing differently.

When your child receives and expresses social information differently, as with autism or developmental delays or even with ADHD, it can leave you feeling dejected, frustrated, and not understanding of how to help your child feel safe and secure. Part of the challenge of parenting an atypical child is in learning to understand your child's mind, or what Daniel Siegel calls "mindsight," the ability to perceive the feelings, thoughts, memories, and meanings for oneself and others. The challenge is to develop your mindsight into how your child's mind works, to see the world as he or she sees it and not to compare your parenting skills with those of a parent of typical children. In fact, research done with parents of children with autism, intellectual disabilities, and language delays, and of neurotypical children has raised the question of just how much a parent needs to adjust their parenting style for atypical children in order to offer their child the basics of attachment: becoming seen as their safe, soothing, and secure haven.[3] The research is still inconclusive; the critical goal of parents to create secure attachment for an atypical child is a necessary, yet at times indefinable and difficult endeavor that must be modified for the needs of a given individual. Again, a good reason to focus on knowing your own particular child and not to become anxious about comparing your parenting experience with that of parents of typically developing children.

For parents of atypical children, how, when, and for how long to be fully sensitive to their child's emotional needs is an area that has not been fully researched. Since atypical children need more tending for longer periods of time, parents' nerves can begin to fray as the daily demands do not diminish as expected, nor does their child respond in predictable or gratifying patterns. What happens when the demand to be available, responsive, and sensitive to a child's needs becomes so overly taxing and continues for so long that the parent starts to feel oppressed and becomes depressed? Isn't that detrimental to the child?

Many parents feel guilty if they suspect that they are not doing enough to create the optimal attachment conditions, covering what Daniel Siegel calls the core four S's: *seeing* the child's needs, *soothing* the child's distress and creating a *safe* haven, which, in turn, creates an internal feeling of *security*. There is no question that this is more challenging with atypical children. And even the most current research is unsure how to properly identify the exact parenting interactions to enhance attachment with atypical children when their social interaction pathways are not as robust. Becoming "over-involved" can happen easily. All atypical children require much more supervision and assistance than typical kids. Over time, the parents' judgment about how much care to provide becomes distorted by stress, doubt about the child's ability to function on his or her own, setbacks, confusion, and conflicting input from spouse and family. Add to that the habitual servitude that comes from the daily demands of keeping up with an atypical child, and it is not hard to see how a parent can become over-involved, if not downright enmeshed in the name of fostering secure attachment. Caring for your child, loving your child, supporting your child—nothing is more important than that, right?

The truth is that care and commitment can turn into something else, a situation where you have lost your sense of freedom, personality, likes, and dislikes—your sense of self. That's too much connection without the important differentiation needed in any relationship. You stop thinking about issues you were once passionate about. Politics, health, career, working out, and socializing are overtaken by obsessively worrying about your child's well-being.

A Dream of Cutting the Cord

Over-involved parents tend to make excuses for their children rather than encouraging them to grow and care for themselves, to whatever extent they can. The parents have lost the ability to tell the difference between what the child can and cannot do. They have become habituated to being on call 24/7. It hobbles the child and can leave the parent feeling dead inside.

My client, Bethany, knows the feeling well. "I've always felt like I had a stone on my chest," she says. Her son Andy, who is a now a young adult, was diagnosed with bipolar disorder as a child and schizophrenia in his teens. Andy was always an impulsive and headstrong child. "He needed constant supervision just to keep him alive," Bethany recalls ruefully.

After Andy was diagnosed, he would take his meds to control his rapidly shifting moods and his parents would take antidepressants to control their despair at being utterly engulfed by caring for him. "I was thinking for him, I was planning for him, and it sometimes felt like I was breathing with him. I could predict what he was thinking and even when his mood might be changing. He wasn't always willing to take medication, so we were always nervous for him, always at the end of our rope." Toward the end of Andy's senior year in high school, Bethany had a dream:

> I was standing on the bank of a rapid river and Andy was in the
> water, eager to swim down the roaring current. He was attached

to me with a thick hemp rope. I knew that I needed to detach from him and let him go. But I was so worried—how was he going to make it down the river? In the dream, I remember sawing and sawing off the rope so that he could be set free but then, as he swam down the river, I ran down the bank to a spot where I hoped I would be able to see him land safely.

I woke up gasping for air, knowing that somehow I had to emotionally detach from him, not only to let him figure things out, but so I could reclaim who I was in the spaces between being Andy's mother. It was so hard to negotiate my feelings and to feel entitled to them. After all, how could I be depressed and feel that life was difficult? Look at what Andy was going through and the life of struggle he had ahead of him. His nightmare was my nightmare too.

It is a delicate balance, being attached just enough while still claiming your own sense of self. Through the many long days, months, and years, it is easy to get worn down to the point where you *are* your child, and your child's struggles are your struggles.

In my opinion, this type of parental depression has not been given the serious attention it deserves. While medications, cognitive behavioral therapy, and talk therapy can be helpful, the truth is that parents need to rediscover their own heart space. They need to reclaim their rightful ground, the ground they stood on before this child came to take up so much emotional territory.

A Place to Start: Common Triggers of Parenting-Based Depression

How do you work your way out of the sinkhole of depression when you are over-involved and embroiled in the daily care of your child? A good place to begin is learning to recognize specific events that may trigger your depression. Most parents find that there are three basic types of triggers: *milestones*, *multiple failures*, and *setbacks*. If you

> **Never lose sight of the small gems of moments of victory.**

are alert to these, you can bolster your spirit against them using one or more of the self-care techniques we'll talk about later in the chapter.

Milestones: Highly Anticipated, Highly Disappointing

Seeing the children of your peers meet meaningful milestones may trigger feelings of deep sadness. These milestones could include graduating from kindergarten or elementary school, getting good report cards or making the honor roll, tryouts for competitive sports or school plays, birthday parties, or graduation from high school or college. If your child is not able to pass these milestones along with his or her peers, it brings your child's (and your family's) difference into sudden focus: *There is no way our daughter is ever going to get accepted at the local high school all our neighbors' kids will be going to . . . There is no way I can let my kid go on the annual sleepaway field trip with his class because of his sensory difficulties, bedwetting, and rigid fears of being away from home . . . At our son's graduation, almost all the other students got awards, and we're just grateful he didn't get expelled for his off-the-charts ADHD and oppositional defiant behaviors.*

At these times, you may feel as if your shortcomings as a family are thrust into the spotlight for all to see. Maybe your friends are not the kind to thoughtlessly gloat about their children, but most proud parents do share their children's achievements, much to your inner dismay that those kinds of triumphs are not within your child's grasp. But you must remember that your child has lots of triumphs as well. Maybe not the kind that other parents would understand, but triumphs just the same. Never lose sight of the small gems of moments of victory.

Multiple Failures: Everyone Fails Sometimes, But Sometimes It Feels Like Too Much

Once again, you get a call from your child's school. And once again, the expressions on the teachers' faces are easy to read. "We don't think we can teach your child in a way that she needs," they may tell you. It's a rejection and a feeling of failure. From your child's doctor: "We have run all the tests, and although we do see that your child is ill, we can't find the right diagnosis and we may never know what is causing this." It's another door slamming in your face. Depression, defeat, and a dead-end feeling are sure to follow. But don't allow those feelings of defeat to engulf you, this too shall pass and you will again feel the delight of breakthroughs and successes.

Setbacks: When Progress Goes Backward— It's Temporary but It Hurts!

Your child may be making progress (or it appears that way to you), only to falter and revert to earlier behavior or stumble over the same problem you thought was finally behind you. It could be a monster tantrum when all has been calm for a while, a low score on a test, or another babysitter quitting because it's too hard to take care of your child. Anytime your optimism is slashed, feelings of depression are normal and might be heading your way.

Be of good cheer. Do not think of today's failures, but of the success that may come tomorrow. You will succeed if you persevere; and you will find a joy in overcoming obstacles.

—Helen Keller

Why Your Child Bounces Back but You Don't

Before we explore ways to manage your feelings, it's worth mentioning one more phenomenon that can nudge you deeper into the pit. You may have noticed that after your child throws a tantrum or has a humiliating setback, he seems to recover fairly quickly, while you end up exhausted and sad for hours. As you watch him placidly munching a sandwich an hour later, you find your mood getting even darker. Why?

There are several reasons. Earlier we talked about the human brain's ability to plan and reflect, and previously in this book, we discussed the brain's executive function and how it develops slowly and only reaches maturity in the mid- to late twenties. Your young child does not have the planning and anticipating capacity that you do. He's not worrying about the next time he has a tantrum or fails gym class. But you are. Your brain is constantly scanning the horizon for future events that might impact your child, while he remains blissfully unaware. Watching him casually eat that sandwich may feel like the last straw. Not that you want him to suffer—you don't—but it may add to your feelings of isolation and despair.

There is a neuropsychological element to your response as well. In adults, the part of the brain that gets activated during stress (the vasovagal system) tends to stay stressed even when the event is over. So hours after your child's last nightly tantrum, when he is fast asleep and looking like the angel he really is, your heart is still pounding and streams of cortisol are still flowing. While your cognitive mind knows it is time to relax, the emotional brain is still surging with stress and panic. You are out of balance and cannot easily regroup.

Maggie, parent of a nine-year-old girl with sensory processing disorder, tells a familiar tale:

> Simone had a toothache and I had to take her to the dentist, but she completely fell apart even in the car. She refused to sit in the dentist chair and the dentist couldn't even check her tooth. Simone was completely traumatized, sobbing and scared. We left the office, and I was devastated while Simone cried all the way home. But when we got home, she happily turned to listen to music on her iPad and she became her old self again. As for me, well, it will take some time to recover. I feel yet again emotionally frazzled, defeated, and depressed by the inevitability of this cycle of behavior.

Stories like this one remind me of what parents are up against, the grinding daily challenges that can feel as if they are wearing down your very soul. Don't give in! You can bolster yourself against these waves. The goal is to develop your optimism and resilience, and reclaim your own sense of self. There are proven ways to get there.

Four Ways to Cultivate Emotional Strength

You are in this parenting role for the long haul, so you must find a way to battle depression and sustain your spirit. There are several methods to cultivate your emotional strength that you can learn to develop. This is not an exhaustive list, but four feasible avenues for you to explore. These four techniques are: mindfulness-based cognitive therapy (MBCT), meditation, practicing self-compassion, and cultivating optimism. Each is a way to change how you perceive your situation. They can be tapped any time you're feeling stressed, and they can also be officially scheduled into your day. Over time, practicing these will alter the way your brain responds to stress, including your child's behavior and the reactions of other people.

Mindfulness-Based Cognitive Therapy (MBCT)

When I first heard about mindfulness, I pictured people sitting on cushions meditating in silence for long periods of time. While that may sound wonderful to busy parents (wouldn't it be nice to be in a quiet room for even a brief period of time?), mindfulness is not really about meditating. It's about noticing your feelings without reacting to them, and learning to intentionally shift your perspective. Developed by Dr. Jon Kabat-Zinn, mindfulness-based cognitive therapy (MBCT) can alter brain circuits by teaching you to observe depressive thoughts rather than react to them. Shifting your perspective to slightly detach emotionally from your child gives you the freedom to observe the situation without judgment. This means you can be attuned to your child without being emotionally engulfed in your child's experience. Thanks to the brain's neuroplasticity (its ability to reroute neural pathways), MBCT can enable you to shift your perspective and incorporate that shift at a cellular level.

Recent research has found that parents of children with disabilities who learned a method of MBCT, called mindfulness-based stress reduction, experienced great improvements in anxiety, depression, and insomnia.[4] In fact, it was found to be so successful that a specific curriculum has been developed just for parents of special-needs children. You don't need to attend this specific course to achieve positive results, but the fact that a course has been developed just for parents like you should validate the fact that parents of atypical children do have extensive psychological needs and that there is treatment available that can help.

Some atypical children require twenty-four-hour care and supervision. This places a terrible burden on their parents. By creating emotional space between you and your child, you are actually shoring up the parent-child relationship—attending to your own needs gives you the strength to keep being an effective and nurturing parent. You may wish to read up on this popular method to help you deal with depression. Two books I like are:

The Mindful Way Workbook: An 8-Week Program to Free Yourself from Depression and Emotional Distress, by John D. Teasdale, Mark Williams, Zindel V. Segal, and Jon Kabat-Zinn

Mindfulness-Based Cognitive Therapy for Depression, Second Edition, by Zindel V. Segal, J. Mark G. Williams, John D. Teasdale, and Jon Kabat-Zinn

For more information about the course of mindfulness-based stress reduction, check out the Parent Stress Intervention Program from Vanderbilt University.

Meditation

Meditation can help build mental equanimity and internal calmness. There are several different types of meditation, but all types require a place of quiet and a place to comfortably sit or lie down. In the classic mindfulness meditation, you just let your mind flow from one thought to the next without judging or reacting. In a focused meditation, instead of letting your mind flow, you actually focus on one thought or one sound for an extended period of time. It can be very relaxing, since we are constantly thinking about multiple things at once in our typical day. There are religious meditations and movement meditations. The important thing is to find the one that works for you. You may want to try a meditation class or use a meditation app on your phone to get going.

> *[Slow breathing] is like an anchor in the midst of an emotional*
> *storm: the anchor won't make the storm go away, but it will hold*
> *you steady until it passes.*
>
> —Russ Harris, author and teacher of acceptance
> and commitment therapy

Whether you are new to meditation or already practice, I recommend the exercises in Dr. Elisha Goldstein's books, including *Mindfulness Meditations for the Frantic Parent* and *The Now Effect: How a Mindful Moment Can Change the Rest of Your Life*. They employ mindful reflection, which can combat feelings of depression and defeat. I also suggest you try the following simple exercises:

Before going to bed at night: Take some deep breaths. Close your eyes and consider: What is your favorite image of your child? Maybe it is how he looks when he is asleep, or the joy on his face when you pick him up from school, or the way he laughs when he tells you a joke. Allow yourself to reflect deeply on that image as you fall asleep. Push away the ruminative thoughts and worries about your child. Worrying never changes anything.

Whenever you feel down: Think of five images or sensory experiences that you can focus on when you're really deflated. What brings you joy? Breathing in the salt air at the beach? Dancing with abandon? Going for a walk in the woods? Smelling your baby's hair? Holding your partner in your arms? Bring these to mind when a dark mood threatens to bring you down.

Cultivating Self-Compassion

Here is the crux of the challenge for the parent who is in the depression phase: You are in the midst of one of life's most difficult challenges, raising a child. This child happens to be different. Sometimes it frightens you, sometimes you don't understand what to do, and sometimes no one has any answers for you. It is a rough and lonely road. No one is holding your hand; you are the grown-up here.

You are worthy and you are ready.

Allowing yourself to feel compassion for yourself—to pat yourself on the back and give yourself kudos for all that you do each day—is not only a kind thing to do, it is essential. Dr. Kristin Neff, researcher on compassion, notes that self-compassion is strongly related to mental well-being, happiness, life satisfaction, and better relationships. Can you imagine how increasing your self-compassion could help you with your relationship with your child as well? You will be a better parent for it. You can direct some of the MBCT and meditation techniques toward self-compassion, for example, by incorporating something you did right, or a difficult task that you accomplished, into your reflections for that day. It also helps if you enlist others to notice what you've achieved. Announce to your family at dinner, "I'm really proud of myself today. Not only did I manage to get Billy to all of his therapy appointments, I cooked us a fabulous dinner! Isn't that great?" (Even if you are the only one cheering yourself on, go for it!)

A natural outgrowth of self-compassion should be to have some designated rewards you regularly give yourself for the mighty and noble job you are doing. Write a list of the experiences that make you feel special, pampered, and appreciated: a massage, tennis lessons, afternoon tea at a fancy hotel, a fishing outing one afternoon with a group of friends. These need to be tangible things that you—*you*—desire. Don't be self-sacrificing about it. A trip to the miniature golf course with your kids doesn't count. (Unless that is the most self-compassionate reward you can think of. Anyone?)

Cultivating Optimism

In *Learned Optimism: How to Change Your Mind and Your Life*, Dr. Martin Seligman describes his research into helping people change their mental set point. If you have a preset tendency toward depression, he says, you can change your outlook by cultivating optimism. Instead of focusing on what's wrong in your life or that of your child, start to focus on what's right. For example, tell yourself: "I have received a diagnosis for my child. I have tried various different treatment options; some have worked, some haven't. Now I am working toward integrating the feasible options into my family's routine. My life and my kid's life are not perfect, but I am doing a good job as a parent, and things are going to get better."

You can also cultivate optimism by making something positive happen—something that has nothing to do with your child. It might be relatively minor, like tending an herb garden on your windowsill, buying a weekly bouquet for your bedroom, or organizing your books into an inviting library. Those small actions will give you a sense of accomplishment, and they can have a cumulative effect.

It takes work to change the emotional tenor of your own mind and heart. We humans do tend to have a negativity bias and get stuck in a mental rut unless we prod ourselves to a more positive frame of mind. The interesting thing is, the more you do it, the easier it becomes. Not only that, you become a role model for your entire household. It's called dyadic regulation; the calm in one person's demeanor can affect and calm other people. Like calmness, optimism is contagious. And wouldn't we all like to spread that around?

> **Optimism is contagious.**

When the Dalai Lama was asked why is he so happy in the face of the terrible pain he has witnessed, he replied, "It is our responsibility to find joy in life, despite the great suffering in the world."[5] In other words, don't let suffering win; don't let life defeat you. You can find the joy despite the incredible burdens. Finding joy trains your brain to find more joy. It's neuroplasticity at its best.

Sometimes your joy is the source of your smile, but sometimes
your smile can be the source of your joy.

—Thich Nhat Hanh

Cultivating Social Support It is tremendously important for all parents to cultivate and experience a web of support around them as they navigate this challenging new road of raising a child. But it is particularly important for parents of atypical children. In the initial stages of learning about your child's condition, you may feel quite isolated. Research has found that isolation makes people more vulnerable to depression, especially isolation related to loss, in this case, the loss of your idealized imagined "perfect" child.[6] Multiple research findings indicate that people, as with other mammals, are literally addicted to being in social relationships and that social interactions actually secrete positive chemicals in the brain similar to strong addictive drugs! It's that powerful. A social network provides comfort that you are not alone, that there are others who are going through what you are going through, maybe not in the specifics but in the overall picture. One thing I guarantee is that no matter what obstacles you are encountering, sharing your experiences with a friend, a thoughtful family member, or a member of a social support network will undoubtedly lift your experience. There are many parents who are experiencing this sense of community and relief of shared experiences through the web, either via Facebook or other social media. Even though Internet communities are so prolific and can be very helpful, I also still endorse the importance of face-to-face group connection in personal real-time encounters.

Your Self-Care Menu

If all you did was put your hand on your heart and wish yourself well, it would be a moment well spent.

—Elisha Goldstein, PhD, psychologist, speaker,
and author of *The Now Effect*

When counseling parents, I help them assemble a customized "self-care menu." The idea is that you brainstorm activities that appeal to you and give them a try in whatever amount you like. You may choose an "appetizer" portion in case you only have fifteen minutes, a "main course" that gives you a larger dose of relief or relaxation, or a "dessert" that you use as reward for a particularly rough day. If you are a full-time working parent, this applies to you as well. In addition to wearing two hats, the home hat and the office hat, you deserve to find some space you can call your own. What would it look like for you?

In putting together your personal self-care menu, you will want to think about your life before you became a parent. What got you out of bed each morning? What was your joy, your favorite hobby, your dream activity? What nourishes your soul, even momentarily? Everyone has interests that can be powerfully healing. Look back and recall the activities that were the most fun or meaningful. Was it laughter and wine with friends? Taking your dog to obedience class? Going to concerts? Cooking a great meal? Playing softball? Repairing bicycles? Playing your guitar? Zumba class? Reading a great novel? Or just having some solitude? Customize the items on your self-help menu so that even reading your list will give you a little lift. Here are the categories that the parents I work with have found to be most helpful.

Connect with Nature

The Japanese have a phrase for the healing effects of nature: *shinrin-yoku* or "forest bathing." Something as simple as taking a walk outside, breathing in the air, and appreciating the wind in the trees can be restorative.

Move Your Body

Look for a physical activity you really enjoy and might even come to crave—riding your bike, dancing, walking, hiking, playing volleyball, boxing. Many people find that it's more fun if you do this activity with a friend or partner. A great many people practice yoga and there is research to support the treatment of depression with specific types of yoga, although you might find ballroom dancing to be more to your liking.

Master Just One Thing at a Time and Then Celebrate It!

If you learn to master just one thing—*that has nothing to do with your child*—it can restore your sense of power. It does not matter what this one thing is; it can be anything from learning to knit to running a marathon. A side benefit to mastering just one thing is that competence at one thing leads to greater competence in other areas of your life. By mastering that one thing, you prove to yourself that you are still learning, growing, becoming.

Find a Special Place for Yourself Outside the Home

All parents should be able to get away from the house and the role of mom or dad, and have a place where they can feel a glimmer of their old selves. Maybe you need solitude and can locate a special meditative spot in a forest or park near your home. Maybe you enjoy your local health club, where you can work out and also connect with other people who aren't necessarily parents. Being outside of your home at a place that is not work related, even for a short burst of time, is invigorating.

Join a Group—Support or Otherwise

Joining or forming a support group comprised of other parents of atypical kids is an excellent way to share experiences and reduce your feelings of isolation. Learning from others about what has helped them will show you that there are more paths toward hopefulness than you may have imagined. If you feel the need for a community of people who are *not* parents, where you can share other interests, that is every bit as legitimate as a support group.

Make Date Night a Top Priority (with Your Partner or Your Friends)

Before you became a parent, you had dates with your partner or your friends. It's time to revive that enjoyable custom.

Help Someone Else

You might think you are burned out with helping, seeing as you are already a caretaker for your child. But I've found in talking to many families that the one thing they are most grateful for is the opportunity to give back. It may seem like a terrible thought to ask you to give even more than you are giving, but the funny thing is, seeing people (or animals) in terrible situations that are different from your own can trigger some positive meaningful feelings inside of you.

Enjoy the Healing Power of Touch

We talked in earlier chapters about the love hormone, oxytocin, and its positive effects on mood. You can trigger the release of oxytocin by getting a massage or by stroking your cat or playing with your dog. Even a pat on the shoulder or a healing hug can be restorative. The comfort of any type of touch seems to generate mood change and ease feelings of loneliness. We are wired to respond positively to the gentle touch of another.

Turning Depression into Reflection

Is it possible that depression can have a beneficial effect? People who have experienced depression are often more reflective, which means they can be better attuned to their own emotions and the emotions of others. They can relate to other people's problems or unhappiness because they've been through dark times themselves.

It makes sense that if you have been depressed and are able to pull yourself out of it, you can bring to the parenting process a more developed sense of attunement and self-reflection, which will greatly benefit your children. The ability to identify and share feelings with your family, along with being a good listener, makes for meaningful communication. I don't mean to imply that it's a good thing to be depressed, but it is a feeling most people will experience at some point in their lives. The same wiring that gives us a tendency toward depression can also be the wiring that creates meaningful relationships, deep reflective conversations, and the language of feeling. And teaching children to be reflective, intuitive, and in touch with their feelings may be an unacknowledged benefit of dealing with the blues.

Psychological pain has a history and . . . it is not a matter of getting rid of it. It is more a matter of how we deal with it and move forward.

—Stephen Hayes and Spencer Smith, *Get Out of Your Mind and Into Your Life*

Andrew Solomon, author of *Far from the Tree*, spent many years researching and interviewing parents of children with differences. He found that people with special-needs children have more compassion for others than is typical. It's a switch you can turn on. And compassion is a key to enhanced mental health. Obviously, parents don't need to be depressed in order to be compassionate or well attuned to their children. But Solomon's work is food for thought, and I have seen in my own practice the connection between the depression phase and greater compassion. Building your level of self-compassion as well as compassion for others seems to have an immunizing effect on one's level of depression, anxiety, and that overwhelmed feeling that can sometime encompass a parent. Dr. Kristin Neff, a pioneer researcher in the field of self-compassion, describes her reaction during a stressful moment in dealing with the tantrum of her son with autism; she said to herself in a moment of panic, "This is so hard right now, darling. I'm here for you." She noted, "I could be openhearted to myself and it helped me be openhearted to Rowan."[7]

The Best Reason to Beat Depression: Your Child

For all the reasons we have talked about in this chapter, it's essential that you recognize when you are depressed. But there is one final reason that may convince you to take action now: Depressed parents affect their children's mental health. The results of many studies have shown that children of depressed mothers are at high risk for depression during childhood and adolescence. They are also at a higher risk for anxiety disorders, social impairment, and alcohol dependence.[8] Depressed parents often try to hide their dark feelings and despondency and suffer in silence, but their children see through it. A recent study found that mothers who disregard their own emotional well-being are inadvertently modeling a flattened or saddened response to life, and their kids absorb and mirror that response.[9]

When parents are asked what they want the most for their children, the universal reply is, "I just want them to be happy." Your children will have a harder time being happy if you are in an ongoing state of depression. And, of course, you owe it to yourself to find joy in your life. Without it, your daily existence becomes increasingly unbearable. Finding joy, feeling good about yourself, and feeling hopeful about your life and your child's life—these are achievable goals for every parent, including those with atypical children.

CHAPTER SIX

Active Acceptance

Joyful and Purposeful Living

I didn't ask for a child with multiple diagnoses, but I adore my son. George was first diagnosed with Tourette's syndrome and ADHD when he was six. He later developed obsessive-compulsive disorder, which made life more difficult for all of us, including George's little sister. We are definitely not a normal family. There are no visits to Disneyland, no family restaurant outings. Every plan requires extra calibration. But it's our normal. A long time ago I decided that I would not allow this to stop each of us from being all we could be, George included. We also have our private family jokes and family traditions and—we also have lots of fun!

In hindsight I realize that we all grew from what could have been considered a difficult situation. We became more aware and sensitive to others who are different, more forgiving, and more compassionate human beings as a result of our atypical challenges. Now I can't imagine our family being different from what it is.

—Lisa, mother of eighteen-year-old George

• • •

What is acceptance, and what exactly are we supposed to accept? Is it simply accepting a particular diagnosis and learning about the best ways to handle it? That's certainly a challenge, and we have discussed the difficulty and the anxiety that it provokes. But active acceptance that takes you to joyful and purposeful living goes beyond passively accepting that your child is atypical. Passive acceptance allows only the cognitive fact to emerge: Your child has a disorder or other condition. Active acceptance integrates both the cognitive and the emotional: Not only do you intellectually acknowledge that a condition exists, you also come to terms with it emotionally and are focused on the options and growth that may be possible.

Getting to that place of acceptance may take months or it may take years. In this chapter, we will talk about the concept of acceptance and share the stories and insights of parents who have learned to walk their atypical path with an open mind and a sense of hope. They have all managed to move past considerable obstacles and do more than just endure their situation. The one thing they have in common is that none would have predicted how their life, and the lives of their family, would eventually unfold.

When I first talk to parents about their child's diagnosis, their thoughts often jump to the future: "Is this a lifelong condition? Will my child be able to grow up and have a relationship? Be successful at a job? Live independently?" When people are anxious, their minds tend to zoom forward in anticipation of the next disaster, where the picture freezes and magnifies. I urge parents at this early stage to stay in the present moment and work their way slowly forward. Otherwise they may become overwhelmed thinking about the years ahead and paralyzed by the enormous reality of the present. The

With acceptance comes unexpected gifts.

truth is, atypical children often need slow unpacking, symptom by symptom, treatment to treatment. Their foundations are built brick by brick. Some outgrow their original diagnoses, but many will mature into adolescents and adults who still exhibit differences. Along the way, parents learn to work through their feelings and adjust their expectations. They learn to accept their child's condition, and with acceptance comes unexpected gifts.

You may wonder how to get to the "gift" stage quickly. There is no express train! Much has to do with intention and retraining your mind, as we explored in earlier chapters. But part of the acceptance process is simply a matter of time—the time it takes you to become more accustomed to your child's condition and your own situation.

The Neuropsychology of Acceptance: Adaptation, Habituation, Desensitization

Our brains are not wired to passively accept alarming challenges. When unanticipated stressors arise, the brain goes into "red alert" mode and the body reacts with a hormonal stress response, continually sending surges of cortisol that can affect your overall health. The brain reacts to stress by triggering physical responses such as elevated blood pressure, faster breathing, and a pounding heart. Since this is not healthy in the long term, the human brain has developed one of its most remarkable skills: adaptation. Over time, the brain adapts to situations that might at first seem tragic or unbearable. This is because our brains are wired to process new information differently than repeated information.

When our brain receives the same information numerous times, it becomes accustomed to it. The novelty-seeking switch is turned off and we respond in a predictable way. With repeated information, we learn optimal responses. At a basic level, this process, known as habituation, relieves our brain from having to rediscover the wheel every time we encounter a familiar situation.

One element of habituation is desensitization. An example would be buying a new clock that chimes every hour. The chime might be startling until you get used to it, at which point it will no longer startle you; in fact, you might not hear it at all. That's why you'll sometimes witness parents of small children who seem to be oblivious to the ear-piercing shrieks of their toddlers in the playground. They *are* oblivious—as long as the children sound happy, they no longer register the pitch of those screams. Other parents may be bothered or embarrassed by their child's shrieks, or they may come from a culture where shrieking is not tolerated. They will continue to hear every shriek and be stressed by it.

In the same way, parents adapt to their child's challenges (the type of challenge and the parent's environment have a lot to do with how quickly or easily parents adapt). Parents become habituated to handling their child's tantrums, extra-long homework sessions, and trips to doctors and therapists. They become desensitized to the tantrums (or less sensitized). They naturally adjust their expectations of their child, so that they aren't anticipating that the homework will be completed quickly. Trips to doctors and therapists become routine. There are fewer surprises, so fewer reasons for alarm. All of these adaptations become their new normal. Adaptation and habituation are natural processes, and will eventually occur without your conscious effort.

However . . .

Peace of mind, calmness, and a capacity for joy and appreciation of your special child requires more than just relying on your brain's built-in adaptation response. To get those positive feelings—and to get to your own version of acceptance—you must learn how to regulate your emotions. It takes work to control your angry, anxious, or negative impulses. It takes conscious effort to rein in your fears about the future. It takes willpower to train yourself to appreciate your child's victories instead of comparing them to what your ideal child might have achieved. What is missing from the natural adaptation response is that it doesn't engage your emotions. Adaptation allows you to survive, function, and take care of your child. A deep awareness of what you are feeling is not necessary to adaptation. You can be a perfectly humming machine on the outside, but on the inside, you may feel like a robot. From a brain perspective, your left hemisphere (the site of facts and linear thinking) is fully engaged, but your right hemisphere (the site of processing feelings, intuitions, and holistic problem solving) is dormant or repressed. I have seen parents who appear dazed and robotic years after their child's diagnosis, adjusting to the routine but not to the emotionally integrated reality of living fully.

Parents who have found growth and joy in their lives because of or despite their child's differences have taken an extra step. They have acknowledged their emotions and have consciously thought about what they want their responses to be—as you have learned to do in previous chapters of this book, and as you can explore further on your own. These parents have made a decision not to squelch the frightening feelings and questions that arise, but to face them honestly and with compassion toward themselves. These questions may include:

- How can I make it better?
- Will it ever be okay?
- How will my social standing be affected?
- Will my extended family blame me or see me as a failure?
- Does this mean I have to be a saint?
- How do I accept myself?
- How do I accept my husband/wife/partner?
- What does this mean for us as a family unit?
- Am I an okay person?
- Will I be able to rise to this challenge?

All parents of atypical children ask themselves questions like these. These questions may not arise in the conscious brain for every parent, but even at a subconscious level, parents do have these types of questions. It takes a while to find the answers and that is part of the work. But the larger part of the work is becoming conscious of the questions and insecurities that you are having and knowing how to take care of yourself in these times of vulnerability. We are all vulnerable. Strength lies not in muscling through but through acknowledging our vulnerabilities, becoming aware of our feelings and honoring them. The ultimate answers are different for every family and individual, and as they are processed, active acceptance can begin to blossom.

> I think our capacity for wholeheartedness can never be greater than our willingness to be brokenhearted. It means engaging with the world from a place of vulnerability.
>
> —Brené Brown, author of The Gifts of Imperfection

Holding Joy and Sorrow in One Heart

Parents of atypical children are often viewed as saints. People marvel, "How do they do it?" The parents tend to respond in one of two ways. It's either "We do it because we have to—please stop glorifying us," or "Our child is a blessing in our life and we wouldn't trade him for anything!" While both are equally valid, the perspectives are different. Having personally known so many of these parents, I can tell you that those with a more positive outlook were not born with a special Pollyanna gene, nor are their children generally less afflicted than others. Sure, some of them may have had an innately optimistic personality before they became parents, but it would be a huge disservice to them to imply that their experience was less traumatic because of that. What is true is that the parents who feel hopeful and blessed make a conscious effort to look for the hope and blessings in their life. That may sound trite, but I assure you it takes as much grit and determination as mountain climbing, only the effort is invisible. You won't get a lean physique from cultivating hope and gratitude, but you will be developing a skill that will serve you—and your family—well.

Most parents of atypical children discover that their hearts can expand to hold joy and sorrow at the same time. Neither emotion disappears for very long. To have a child who is different means that you always carry a small weight on your heart, whether the disorder is severe or relatively minor. Feeling two conflicting emotions at once is not an unusual state—many people experience simultaneous extreme emotions. People can mourn and also celebrate; they can feel deep loss and also profound gratitude. In fact, at times it seems that the deeper the loss, the sweeter the victory. You can learn to mediate conflicting emotions and consciously ask yourself, "Which emotion am I going to go with? Am I going to cry or be joyous? Am I going to see what my child is missing or am I going to rejoice the victories?" Sometimes it helps to say it out loud: "I am sad about my child's challenges *and* I am also so proud of him!" Acknowledge the polarity and allow both feelings to be present. Acknowledge that you are vulnerable emotionally, and embrace yourself compassionately.

Writing in the *Huffington Post*, Liane Kupferberg Carter described her conflicted emotions about raising an autistic son, who is now in his early twenties:[1]

Acceptance doesn't mean giving up, and it isn't a constant state. Grief and anger rear up unexpectedly. Sometimes I still get tired of the relentless effort, the endless round of therapies and team meetings and fights with the insurance companies. This process of healing is a destination without an arrival. Joy and grief are joined in lockstep.

Ultimately, what buoys our family is hope. When I look at him, I do not see "autism." I see my child: an animated, endearing, handsome young man with a mischievous sense of humor. Parenting this trusting, gentle boy has deepened me immeasurably. But would I trade in my hard-earned equanimity and expertise if someone could magically make his challenges go away tomorrow? In a heartbeat.

"Children like ours are not preordained as a gift," one mother explains. "They're a gift because that's what we have chosen."
—Andrew Solomon, *Far from the Tree*

Embracing the Paradox

Acceptance doesn't mean that you're pleased about your child's condition. There is no contradiction between loving someone and feeling burdened, exhausted, angry, or burnt out. All parents confront that paradox. As a parent of an atypical child, you have even deeper contradictions to absorb: fiercely loving your child but absolutely hating what he or she has to endure or the changes it thrusts upon you and your family. This is the basis of dialectical thinking: understanding that polar opposite feelings actually create a coherent and meaningful whole. There is light in every darkness and darkness in every light. It's an embrace of both extremes that create meaning.

Why some people cope with the paradoxes of parenthood better than others is a topic of interest to many researchers, including Dr. Elizabeth Larson.[2] When studying parents of children with disabilities, Larson found that the way mothers express contradictory emotions such as grief and joy, or hope and fear, influences their well-being. The great emotional (and spiritual) challenge is to manage the internal tension between loving your child and wanting to erase the disability, between dealing with the incurability while pursuing solutions, and between maintaining hopefulness for the child's future while being given negative information and battling your own fears. Larson's research found that if parents can accept that this is a paradox, they can gain a greater sense of control and increase their optimism.[3]

One mother described her efforts to manage her fears and feelings about her child and the child's illness: "When my daughter first began having seizures, I had so much anxiety about the future and what it would hold for her and for us, basically I just freaked out. Then I thought about all the grieving families around the world who had lost children through terrible tragedies, and I decided I would learn how to cherish every moment. It wasn't easy . . . As terrifying as my daughter's seizures are, and as helpless as I feel whenever she has one, even in those moments, I try to remember how blessed we are to have been given this special little person."

Another mother says, "I never imagined the doors that having a child with spina bifida could unlock for me. My love for Sophie knows no bounds, but the gift in this situation was something totally unexpected. Our family has grown closer, our capacity for empathy has expanded, and our other children have an extra measure of compassion and social awareness that typical families don't have."

As you move past the sorrow, the denial, the anger, and the self-judgment, you can arrive at a place of gladness and acceptance—of your child and yourself. This doesn't mean that the difficulties go away; it means that suffering and joy can coexist. On your path toward acceptance, perhaps there is an ideal frame of mind to which you can aspire, where your internal conversation might sound something like this:

Okay, I get it. This is who he is and this is who I am. He is not perfect; neither am I. I will do my very best to help my child on his journey to adulthood. Sometimes I will feel overwhelmed. Sometimes I will be angry. Sometimes I will still feel sad. My feelings will never go away. And that's okay. Insight and understanding are half the battle. I will remember to take care of myself and my needs, and I will be mindful of when I am nearing the end of my patience. Just as my child needs extra care, so do I. I will make sure to get what I need for myself so that I can be the best person I can be.

Living with Uncertainty, Letting Go of Expectations

No one can predict the future or know how life will unfold, even in the next moment. So one way to talk about acceptance could be summed up in two words: Accept uncertainty. Accept that for your child, acquired skills may come at different stages and levels than they do for other children. And despite every effort, every intervention, every therapy and treatment, progress may take time. Accept that progress may not come the way you anticipate, and there may be forks in the road that you and your family will need to navigate.

Acceptance doesn't mean that you have gained control of the situation. Some things you will be able to work with, some things you will find intolerable. Some things will change while other things will not. Accepting your child's differences does not diminish the struggle, nor does it take away the anxiety about whether or not your child will turn out okay. All the implications of your child's atypical profile may not become clear for a long time, but meanwhile, cultivating optimism and choosing to be joyful is the one thing within your power to do that absolutely will help you, whatever the future holds.

A main theme of this book—letting go of expectations—is critical to acceptance. The sooner you let go of your expectations, the sooner you will be able to find and embrace the life you are meant to lead. The mother of a severely ill two-year-old born with a genetic disease explained it like this: "If we expect that every child is going to be 100 percent perfect, that it's an automatic right that goes along with our expectation, it opens us up to grief. Once the expectation is adjusted, many paths become viable. Dropping the expectation opens the door to humility and to letting go of the pretense of control—*I am not the one who runs the world.* Then you don't feel the sense of loss, except for the loss of your ego. When you let go of your ego, you are released from your burden; this is true freedom. I have faith that there is something greater than us that controls the planet, who supports us and gives us what we have. We come into this world with our nature and neurological wiring. Nurture only can do so much."

The sooner you let go of your expectations, the sooner you will be able to find and embrace the life you are meant to lead.

What Will the Neighbors Say?

Many parents report that they would be able to reach a place of acceptance more easily were it not for having to deal with well-intentioned but hurtful outsiders: teachers, neighbors, health professionals, passersby, relatives. One study found that many parents reported a "shared consciousness of sorrow" but told of an important revelation.[4] The sorrow they experienced originated largely from having to deal with recurring messages of negativity from other people who have not yet learned to embrace the diversity of differences in our society. Despite the unanticipated amount of challenges in having an atypical child, these parents might manage quite well, with optimism and resourcefulness, were it not for outsiders adding stress and negativity about their child.

Other research has found that a parent's perception of his or her child may be affected by social and cultural beliefs about the child's condition. Different societies have different cultural norms, and some are still intolerant or uninformed about different types of disorders. As the number of atypical children increases and more people are open about their differences, it may become easier for parents of all backgrounds to weave more seamlessly into the social fabric. Parents should never have to worry about being shunned by their community because of their child's condition. Yet even in modern and well-educated communities, many parents secretly feel ashamed of their atypical child's behaviors or lack of prowess in academics or sports. Worrying that your child may cause you and your family to be shut out of the community makes the whole concept of acceptance painful and complicated. You may love your child with all your heart but refuse to fully acknowledge his or her condition because you fear the isolation it may bring.

That is why some parents resist certain medical diagnoses, as we have seen in earlier chapters. The medical label confirms that there is something wrong, even though the label may also be the key to getting the child crucial support and services. The official diagnosis—autistic, dyslexic, ADHD—may temporarily obstruct your view of the complex person your child actually is. Outsiders' reactions to the diagnosis may reinforce your feelings of alienation. Part of acceptance is regaining your ability to see your child as an individual human being with challenges and also with potential, regardless of the label and regardless of other people's reactions and cultural expectations.

The need to belong to a group is a strong human drive. But belonging doesn't mean conformity. In fact, it is only when you are open to the outside world about who you are that you will be able to feel comfortable socially. If you worry that people will think less of you because of your child's condition, those are not true friends. If you worry that your family will not be accepted within a particular group or religious circle because of your child, find a group with whom you can be open. This may be a scary, uncomfortable part of your family's journey, but it will lead to a community where your whole family is accepted and everyone can feel at ease.

Resilience and Transformation:
Growth Through Crisis

Most parents are surprised to discover how resilient they are when their child's future and well-being depend on it. Resilience once was seen as an extraordinary quality that only a few heroic figures possessed, but recent studies show that most of us have the potential to cultivate this life-enhancing trait. We all have reserves that go much deeper than we know. And beyond resilience is yet another layer of personal development: transformation.

> *Resilience is accepting your new reality, even if it's less good than the one you had before. You can fight it, you can do nothing but scream about what you've lost, or you can accept that and try to put together something that's good.*
>
> —Elizabeth Edwards

Many people have heard about post-traumatic stress disorder (PTSD), but a less well-known phenomenon is post-traumatic growth. This refers to the positive changes that may occur, or that people may choose, after experiencing a crisis or trauma. Although these people have certainly suffered, they are able to grow from crisis rather than get crushed by it.[5] Viktor Frankl, a psychologist who survived the holocaust and the loss of his family, wrote many books, including *Man's Search for Meaning*. In this seminal reflection on spiritual survival, Frankl described his experiences in concentration camps and how they ultimately led him to develop further meaning in his life. "What is to give light, must also endure burning," he wrote.

Researchers have found that there are people who grow from struggling with crisis even while experiencing personal stress. Finding benefit—indeed, experiencing personal growth—through crisis is never a voluntary mission. It occurs only in retrospect, as you look over your shoulder to measure the path you have walked. Yet knowing in advance that there is the possibility of growth can make you more optimistic as you are raising your child. Life is uncertain, but the uncertainty can hold unexpected treasures. The you that emerges from this experience may have talents, skills, and wisdom that never would have developed had you not walked though these flames. But as Frankl stresses, you must choose to nurture your new strengths: "Forces beyond your control can take away everything you possess except one thing, your freedom to choose how you will respond to the situation."

Many parents stay in survival mode and are satisfied with that. Others do a complete 180 in their lives and become high-profile advocates for their child's disease or condition. But even if you don't create your own foundation or set the world ablaze in awareness of your child's affliction, knowing that you have grown into a stronger, more compassionate person can surely be a source of solace.

Resilience (bouncing back from crisis) and transformation (growth because of crisis) are priceless strengths that may emerge from your experience. The following have also been found to increase for many people who have experienced personal growth through crisis:

- Improved relationships
- Feeling new possibilities for their own life
- Greater appreciation of life in general
- A greater sense of one's personal strength
- Spiritual development
- A greater sense of compassion for others who are in difficult situations[6]

People who experience growth through crises will still face emotional stress or feelings of vulnerability. Growth doesn't inoculate you from pain, but it does give you the confidence that you can live through it and continue to thrive.

Resilience Times Two: A Mother and Son Teach Each Other

One of the first families I ever worked with was a mother and son, Nava and Timor. Timor was already a teenager when I met them, and Nava told me about the frustrations of raising a little boy with severe ADHD and oppositional defiant disorder during the 1980s, when far less was understood about those conditions.

Despite the fact that the family was well-to-do, the lack of awareness about Timor's disorders left them with nowhere to turn for advice. The mother was desperate for support, but she got none. Timor's differences embarrassed her Old World extended family, and her husband thought Timor just needed more discipline. With help from no one else, Nava and Timor forged ahead as best they could. Nava told me, "I always accepted Timor for who he was and I always believed in him, even in my darkest time. I would see glimmers of who he was going to be while he was growing up. The gentle way he handled the new puppy, the way he stood up against a bully who had it out for the nerdy neighbor kid. I used these as shreds of evidence that Timor was going to be okay. And I looked for signs of growth. I never stopped looking."

Nava's life felt like a war zone sometimes, but ultimately she realized that she was also gaining strength—belief in herself as a woman and belief in her abilities to accomplish difficult tasks. When Timor was sixteen, Nava started her own catering business. This stressed-out, exhausted, and at times depressed mom, who had worked tirelessly to care for her son, shifted her energy to another direction. One of her passions was food, and with the support of a cousin, she was able to launch her enterprise. She moved from seeing herself as a victim of her son's disability to being a businesswoman with the emotional resources to sustain her catering firm in a competitive market.

Timor now works with her at the catering company. With his knowledge of social media and franchising, he helped her develop her brand and become established in the food industry.

Today, at twenty-five, Timor is a sturdy and energetic young dad. Nava told me that shortly after his own son was born, Timor threw his arms around her and said, "Thank you for never giving up on me! I don't know where I would have been if you hadn't stood by me while I was growing up."

Another mom, whose son has high-functioning autism, reminded me that acceptance is a steady, ongoing process. Her son, now thirty-five, was a source of both pride and anxiety until he was in his twenties. She wrote, "Being a father really matured him more quickly than I ever could. He is an exceptional father and spends a lot of time with his wife and child. He is holding a job in a computer tech service . . .

"When does acceptance happen? Slowly, over time. You've got to work with what you've got, rather than what you think you want or what you think you should have. It was only along the way that I learned to drop my expectations and to develop a life for myself, as well as help my son. . . . Here is what I learned: No one is normal and no one has a perfect life. And as amazing as your child is, and as much as you love him, making time for yourself will make you a better parent, and he will be better for it too."

The Risk of Crash and Burn

Active acceptance isn't about achieving a blissful state of rapture or an all-enduring high. It's more like a slow but steady evolution. Active acceptance emerges when you consciously work toward making life positive and fulfilling despite your child's differences, or in many cases, because of them. Many families do adapt quite well, building the type of resilience and coping skills that turn the tide from despair to empowerment.

However, all the questions parents ask when they first receive their child's diagnosis—"Is this a lifelong condition?" and the other concerns about the years ahead—are definitely worth contemplating once you have reached the acceptance phase. When parents have extra burdens that will last indefinitely, they need to make realistic plans for the future. This means planning how you are going to take care of yourself, not only for your child's sake, but also so that when your child grows up you will still have a self separate from your identity as a parent.

Some parents appear to be thriving as they raise their atypical child, only to go through an entirely different and surprising set of emotions once the child leaves home. I call this the crash-and-burn phenomenon. Parents are wired to maintain optimal functioning while their children are in their care—they work quite well in rescue mode. Juggling the demands of a home, their child, and a business or job leaves them in a state of perpetual multitasking. Filled with a daily sense of purpose from caretaking, they see little room for any "extras," such as tending to their own needs or dreams. But parents who continue on overdrive for eighteen years or more may not recognize themselves at the end of the journey.

I have seen firsthand what can happen when parents are so single-mindedly focused on their child that everything else falls by the wayside. The cost: losing yourself and perhaps your relationship with your partner. This is a risk for any two people raising children together, and it is the subject of countless books. But it's different for parents of atypical kids. There is no countervailing cultural wisdom you can trust about how much parenting is too much. Those moms at your kid's school who think you're a helicopter parent? They're clueless about how much help your child actually needs. So who's to say what the limits of your involvement should be?

The answer is, you will have to make those calls and set those boundaries yourself, but it can be extremely difficult. In their determination to leave no stone unturned, some parents never stop advocating for their child. They form or attend workshops and support groups, fundraising events, and awareness-raising efforts. Their community becomes ever more centered on their child's condition. Their friends consist of other families with similarly affected children. Their leisure hours are spent researching new treatments, facilities, or opportunities for their child. All these activities may feel right—they fit into the emotional bucket labeled "I'll do everything I can to help my kid." What's missing for your child is a role model of well-rounded, reasonably content, somewhat relaxed adult behavior.

Also missing may be the model of a loving relationship between two adults. The number of divorces among families of children with special needs is exorbitantly high. We've seen throughout this book how the challenges of raising atypical children can bring their parents closer together or, too frequently, drive them apart. Nourishing your partner and being a support system together is a hidden necessary challenge. At the very least, try to remember to occasionally look your partner in the eye and say, "How can I be there for you?" as well as "Here are some things I need to have in our relationship."

While some parents find deep fulfillment in caring for their special-needs child, there are pitfalls. Many well-meaning and energetic parents eventually burn out. While your child is busy evolving into a young adult and beyond, you too should be evolving. The surprise of being an adult is that adulthood also has phases of growth. Adults of all ages continue to develop personal habits, cultivate tastes, refine their palates, and grow their community. Along the way, they make choices. Sometimes they're too busy to reflect on those choices. Has the person who shares a carpool with you become your best friend simply because you see each other every day? Have you neglected date night with your spouse because it's too hard to get a babysitter? Is your community comprised only of families with atypical children? Have you become a 24/7 super-parent?

Super-parents are the ones most likely to crash and burn, and it's sad, because often their efforts have been quite successful—for their kids. But I also know a lot of parents who have learned to balance their own needs against those of their children, and who have raised resilient, well-adjusted young adults. Those young adults do not have to wonder if their condition was an excessive burden on their parents. They grew up seeing their parents involved in interests and friendships that were separate from their child. These adult children have the emotional freedom that comes from knowing that their parents' happiness does not depend entirely on how well they, the children, are doing.

When your time for being a hands-on parent draws to a close, will your children feel confident that they, and you, will be okay? Naturally you will grieve a bit; all parents do when their children leave the nest. Naturally you will worry. But if you plan right now to put your own needs and mental health somewhere on your priority list, you will be in a much stronger place ten or twenty years from today.

More than a Garden: A Place for Parents to Grow

Sabina and Tomas credit Sabina's sense of survival for restoring balance to their lives and getting them to a place of active acceptance. Both parents knew that their son, Phillip, was different from an early age. He was too intense, too active, and too emotional. Phillip didn't get a diagnosis until his late teens, but Sabina was an advocate for him from kindergarten forward. When he was nine, she went back to work full-time. It was not easy; in fact, it was exhausting. Without a diagnosis, Sabina and Tomas had nothing to rely on but their instincts and endless hours of Internet research, which they did at night.

When Phillip entered middle school still without a diagnosis, Sabina took a hard look at the years that lay ahead. She recalls thinking, "Wait a minute. I'm putting all my energy into him. What about me? What about Tomas? Something has to change, and it doesn't look like it's going to be our son. It'll have to be me."

Sabina continued to be a strong advocate for Phillip, but she started to investigate outlets for her own energy and creativity. Her backyard, a city rectangle of grass and concrete rubble, had always intrigued her. What could she do with it? She began to read gardening magazines while waiting in carpool lines and at doctor offices. She cultivated ideas about her own garden. One Saturday she asked Tomas to help her, and they started picking up pieces of concrete rubble from the yard. They started to dig. And plant.

Over time, the garden became a wonderland of exotic plants, antique furniture, reflecting mirrors, and umbrella-shaded nooks. Together the couple visited flea markets and nurseries and bought small objects or unusual plants to bring home. They worked on their garden every Saturday, when their son spent time with his grandparents. Within a few years, the garden became a magnet for their friends.

It was Tomas who discovered meditation and set up an area full of shady plants, little sculptures, and a flowing fountain where he could practice. When his son's challenges threatened to overwhelm his emotional resources, Tomas would retreat to the garden and dig a little, sit and listen to music, or meditate. When he felt more composed, he would return to the challenge at hand. After a while, Sabina got curious about meditation and joined Tomas in a daily practice, starting early before the kids woke up. Word spread among their friends, and people would stop in for a shared meditation practice in the yard.

Sabina and Tomas have turned down offers to develop a landscape design business, deciding that they are content for now. The garden and meditation have become a joint passion and an outlet for their creative energy. This is what acceptance is like for them: a place of balance and peace to offset the demands of outside life.

In his final year of high school, Phillip was diagnosed with bipolar disorder. The challenges of atypical parenting are never over, but Sabina and Tomas are now experts at balancing active participation in their child's challenges with their own interests. "There comes a time when you are ready to cross the line back into your own life," Sabina says. "Helping your child is not your entire life. Don't waste it."

Self-Care Over the Long Run

Most of the discussion in this book has been about helping you manage different emotional phases and daily parenting challenges, which will change as your atypical child gets older but will always

> Compassion for yourself is wind in your sails.

be there in some form. My hope is that you can learn to care for yourself as you care for your child, maintaining a patient, positive, and optimistic outlook every day and also in a deeper sense.

The deeper level of self-care is a long-term plan for nurturing your personal growth, emotional balance, and relationships with other people. However, it will be hard to do this unless you genuinely feel that you deserve it—in other words, unless you feel compassion for yourself. We touched on this subject in the last chapter and I want to expand on it here, because after working with parents and their children for most of my adult life, I can honestly say that it is the hardest lesson for parents to learn. They come into my office completely focused on their child and think, "As long as I'm taking care of my kid, I'm okay." But the truth of this book and the truth of your journey from diagnosis to acceptance is that unless you acknowledge your own vulnerability and develop your ability for self-compassion, your growth as a parent will not fully be complete. Guilt and self-blame are heavy stones in your boat as you row down this river. Compassion for yourself is wind in your sails. So let's take a look at why it's so hard for parents to accept themselves, to forgive themselves, to praise themselves—to love themselves as much as their children love them.

Continued Reflections on Self-Compassion

All women and men come to parenting with their own unique background, assumptions, and expectations. They also come with their own history of diagnoses and disorders. Parents were also children, and they were parented, and they may have had (perhaps undiagnosed) learning disabilities, autistic behaviors, anxiety, or physical health challenges that affect the way they parent.

In addition, every set of parents is unique. Each relationship and set of circumstances is unique. So when I first meet a child's parents, I am aware that there are more than two people in the room. There is also the relationship between them, and all the people in both of their backgrounds. There is the immediate community and the larger culture, standing like an invisible crowd behind them.

And that is a big part of the reason self-compassion is so difficult. All parents arrive at my office with an intricate history, and because of that, they may react to a diagnosis—or to a treatment plan or even to their child—in ways that are surprising and dismaying to themselves. Just as their expectations have been disrupted, their reactions are also disrupted. They may be hostile, upset, or volatile. They may shut down and become removed and cold. It all depends on how they are wired, and no one knows how they're wired until they are in a situation that tests their wiring. They may behave entirely differently than they ever have before, and not in a good way. So from the get-go, parents may be disappointed in themselves, or even appalled, and that works against self-compassion.

Rigid Families and Chaotic Families:
Obstacles to Self-Compassion

While every family's situation is different, I have seen that many parents of atypical children have child-rearing styles that are either extremely rigid or overly chaotic. Both styles can lead to parents blaming themselves for the family's difficulties, and self-blame is the opposite of self-compassion.

The rigid families are those who try too hard to be perfect. They agonize over every detail, have extremely high expectations, and are excessively rigid in their approach to life and their definition of success. This mindset all but guarantees that someone (therapists, schools, the child, themselves, or each other) will come up short. Compassion for others or yourself has little hope of thriving in that harsh environment. I tell them to remember this phrase and tape it to their refrigerator:

Perfection Is Out of Our Reach

The Serenity Prayer is especially meaningful for rigid parents of atypical kids: *God, grant me the serenity to accept the things I cannot change, the courage to change the things I can, and the wisdom to know the difference.* Perfection is always out of our reach, but nevertheless, we can grow. Self-growth may not lead to perfection, but it is an essential part of healthy human development.

> *Nothing's perfect, the world's not perfect. But it's there for us, trying the best it can, and that's what makes it so damn beautiful.*
> —Hiromu Arakawa, *Fullmetal Alchemist*, Vol. 1

For parents who come from excessively rigid frameworks, my advice is to step back and take a broader view. Too often, their idea of success is measured in quantifiable increments, such as neat rooms, homework assignments completed, and bedtime schedules met. I often need to guide these parents in how to develop compassion for their child and decrease their expectations. More cuddling, more fun, and less focus on accomplishments go a long way toward increasing this type of family's joie de vivre. That leads to a more relaxed, happier family and higher level of well-being for everyone.

The situation with chaotic families is a little more complicated. These parents are chronically overwhelmed by life. Although they are typically more "fun" than the rigid families, they may have difficulty maintaining the type of productive structure that will help their child. The parents themselves often struggle with self-regulation. They may come from chaotic families of origin; they may yell at each other, their house may be a mess. Chances are, their child will also struggle with emotional regulation, organizing him- or herself, and sticking to daily schedules.

I often see this in families where the children have ADHD, which is largely genetic. I can pull out a prescription pad and write, "Dinner at six o'clock. Homework at seven. Bath at eight. At eight-thirty, child in bed." But parents have feelings, they have limited capabilities, they are human. They may have a very hard time providing that type of care. When I work with families like this, the first thing I do is address the most overlooked but most important question: *Do you think you will be able to handle this?* To get even more specific, I ask:

Do you have issues similar to the ones I described about your child?

How are you feeling about hearing your child's diagnosis?

Do you want to add some thoughts to this conversation?

How can I help you process and utilize this information?

Parents are rarely asked about their ability to comply with treatment plans. They are often given a cursory diagnosis or a long report that is confusing, and they understandably can feel lost. When they can't follow through on the plan, that's more self-blame. In short, they are set up for failure, which makes it all the harder for them to feel good about and compassionate toward themselves. I hope that professionals who are reading this will realize that providing clinical expertise is only part of the job. The rest lies in their ability to clearly explain treatment plans and be compassionate to parents as well as to their littlest patients.

Self-Blame: "I Don't Deserve Compassion!"

Another major obstacle to developing self-compassion is the tendency of parents to blame themselves for their child's condition. I talked about this in an earlier chapter, and I bring it up again here because it is so corrosive to a parent's spirit. I constantly hear parents tormenting themselves about their stressful jobs, what discipline they used when the child was young, or what they could have done wrong that caused their child's problems. It bears repeating: You cannot change whatever happened in the past, but you can look forward. Forgive yourself, if you can, for your perceived sins.

I realize that you may rationally grasp that your child's condition is not your fault and yet still feel bad, guilty, and as if there is no way to ever make up for what's happened. You may feel that your emotional pain must match whatever pain your child is going through, even though you know intellectually that this won't help you or your child. I understand too that there is only so much this or any book can do to convince you to forgive and feel compassionate toward yourself. If guilt and self-judgment are preventing you from taking self-care steps that you know would benefit you and (by extension) your child, please consider seeing a therapist who can support you and help you develop a more positive self-image.

Remember too that modeling self-compassion is one of the most valuable gifts you can give your child. All children, but especially those who are atypical, have a tendency to be hard on themselves and blame themselves for their parents' worry and unhappiness. You—*only you*—can teach your child by example that every human being is lovable and worthy of kindness. You can teach your son or daughter that it is normal and expected to be kind to yourself, to forgive yourself, to have realistic expectations of yourself.

Survive and Thrive: A Lifelong Plan

We all know that it takes a village to raise a child. With atypical kids, it takes an army. So after self-compassion, the most important thing to learn is that you can't do this alone. I'd like to share with you the following time-tested ways to assemble your support team for the years ahead.

Cultivate Your Extended Family

Having a child will change your relationship with family members, especially your parents. A relationship that was rocky throughout your teens and distant in your twenties can very quickly shift when your focus is different. Just as you are not merely a daughter or son any longer, your mom and dad are no longer just parents. They have another role, as grandparents, so don't assume that they are the same people who raised you. Consider the possibility too that they might be eager for a reason to connect with you in a different way. This child might be the bridge that allows them to express their love for you, regardless of your rocky past relationship.

Your siblings are another potential source of support. What might have been rancorous sibling rivalry can evolve into something altogether different if your brother or sister wants to be an aunt or uncle to this child. You may see a side of this person that you never noticed before. Or they may develop an empathy and generosity of spirit they didn't know they possessed. This is a recurring theme among the families with whom I work.

Become Part of a Community, Whether It's Religious, Political, or Cultural

Although this suggestion may make some people uncomfortable, the research backs it up: Children who grow up in a faith-based community and feel embraced and welcomed by that community are emotionally better off.[7] If you are an atheist or agnostic, consider a cultural or secular group that has the same community-focused features as a spiritual organization. The goal of raising any child is to enable him or her to become integrated in the larger community. Religious or cultural communities can help atypical kids gain confidence, mingle with other children and adults, and learn how to contribute their effort to the group. There are a lot of obvious benefits for parents, too. If you are not the joining type, try to develop new relationships that can nurture and support your family within a group setting. Even joining a local political grassroots organization that makes the world a better place can be inspirational on a personal and family level.

Find Your Community of Friends and Be a Friend

Having supportive friends at this stage of your life is critical. The nonjudgmental friend who brings over dinner when you're falling apart. The friend who's going to take your kids for a walk with your dog so you can go take a shower, or the friend who will come over at the drop of a hat to have a cup of coffee with you when you're just feeling lonely. Loneliness, isolation, being overwhelmed, needing a break—these are all issues that parents with atypical kids really struggle with. Build lifelines to other people who you feel understand your situation and can help support you. There is truth to the saying that in order to get a good friend, be a good friend, so remember to give to others and nourish your dear relationships with your friends, colleagues, or members of your community. Consider joining an advocacy group or support group for families with atypical children. Adding to your community allows for new opportunities to offer and receive support.

Create the Possibility for Sexual Intimacy with Your Partner

Relationships struggle when all the adult energy goes into making sure the kids are all right. It starts with personal care and creating a small space that is yours, a corner of your world that allows for lighting a scented candle, playing your type of music or taking a long bath. One can't offer intimacy to the other if their own self isn't nurtured; there is simply not enough to go around!

If there's one thing parents hate to hear, it's, "Sex! Use it or lose it!" How fair is that when it's three in the afternoon and you haven't gotten out of your sweats or taken a shower and your hair is stringy and you're dealing with tantrums and you've got to jump in the car and race your kid over to see the therapist? Outside messages can start to torture you, like *use it or lose it*. Instead, start looking inward at what rings your bell. What does it take for you to build up more intimate energy to share?

Intimate relations with your partner may lose their place on your priority list when you're worried about your child, but you also may have forgotten how fun and gratifying they are and how they can nourish your relationship. Starting from a place of compassion and curiosity about yourself, ask yourself what it would take to get you in the mood. It could be a three-day buildup. Would you like to get your nails done? Would you like time to soak in a bath? What would make you feel desirable? You can probably get yourself in the mood under the right circumstances. Now that you're a parent, you may not have intimacy opportunities as often as you used to, but I'm sure many people reading this would settle for once or twice a month.

To restart (or improve) intimate relations with your partner, try making it into a ritual. That may go against our culture's romantic fantasy about great sex being wild and impulsive, but most parents quickly learn that *wild* and *impulsive* are words that now apply to their children, not their sex life. Shared sunset walks, the pleasure of a good movie, dancing to your favorite music after the kids are in bed—now those are all good activities leading to shared intimate moments.

Communicate with your partner, reaffirming the importance of your relationship, and focus on the pleasure that comes from being together. Communicating about your relationship may feel uncomfortable. Still, it helps if your partner is aware of your intentions: "Sweetheart, I love you, and what is it going to take to get us both in the mood? Here is what I need, and what do you need?"

There's no shame in thinking honestly about what you need and what it will take in order for you to desire a sexual connection with your partner. While sexuality is not typically thought about as being part of parenting, it is an important part of adult lives and does not need to become extra unresolved baggage, as you grow to become the best parent you can be.

Single parents also need to find and develop intimacy on an adult level. If one's primary role is a parent, it is important to remind yourself that you have important adult needs that are not going to be met within the parenting sphere. So take that leap and think about dating or expand the possibilities to feel sexually alive and desirous.

Learn How to Work with the School System or Social Services System in Your Area

Working with the system is an important part of your personal journey. It can be incredibly depressing and frustrating to feel that the social system that should be helping your child is letting you down. This can make you feel personally ineffective and has a great deal to do with whether you feel you are succeeding or failing with your child. Yet you can learn ways to more effectively work with the system, which can empower your family and other families in your community.

There is no way to avoid the fact that navigating the school and social service system will be an essential part of your job as a parent. It's probably one of the most difficult jobs you will have, but getting the right type of services for your child is worth the energy and the fighting sometimes makes the difference. My advice is: *Do not back down from what you think your child needs.* Never take no for an answer. If you start to feel defeated, hire an advocate or go see a lawyer. If that lawyer fails you, go see another lawyer. If that is outside your means, consult with an advocacy group. There are people who can help—please take the time to find them.

It's no secret that many city, county, and state governments do a terrible job of meeting the needs of children who are different. Unless parents keep fighting for their children, the system will stay apathetic, bureaucracy-bound, and ineffective. Remember that the people in charge of decision making do not have a vested interest in your child but are working from a more pragmatic, big-picture view. Try to work with them but don't try too hard to accommodate them. The system needs to accommodate your child. Do everything you can so that they take the needs of your child seriously.

Taking It to the Next Level

Working hard for your child and caring for yourself is going to take up the majority of your time when your child is young, but eventually, as things fall into place—or maybe even when things aren't exactly in place but are pretty good—you will wonder, *What's next?*

We have talked much about your feelings, but an important part of adult development is meaning and engagement. Active acceptance does not mean slowing to a halt—"I've done good, now I can sit back and relax." Relaxation is terrific and essential, and you more than deserve it. But it may not be entirely satisfying.

As the parent of an atypical child, you are becoming an expert on your child's condition. Every step you take, every experiment you try (including the ones that don't work) make up a body of information you can use to help other parents, teachers, and therapists. Your parenting experience might feel like an isolating one right now, but at some point it will be your turn to inspire, to educate, to share, and perhaps even to lead. As you develop an appreciation of your child as the gift that he or she is, I hope you will also recognize and appreciate what a great parent you are becoming.

You have wept and mourned, you have celebrated and connected, you have had your share of failed attempts and successes. Maybe you could have lived without quite so many disappointments, but it all adds up to a store of knowledge that you alone possess. Are you ready to take your show on the road, to volunteer, to help others, to share information? If your answer is "no," can you make it "not yet"?

Wherever you are in your journey, remember that "good enough" is often as good as it gets. When you have let go of your expectations, tuned in to your feelings, and learned to feel compassion for yourself, those around you, and especially for your child, you may find that beyond acceptance lies an unexpected blessing. Being the parent of a special child does not have to become your sole identity—whatever your passions were before you became a parent may always play a major role in your life. But parenting such a child will change you profoundly, and I encourage you to stay open to the places this experience may lead.

Called to Make a Difference

Many parents of atypical children have gone on to become spokespersons for their children's disorders. Jim and Nancy Abrahams, whom we met in Chapter 4, created the Charlie Foundation, which they continue to promote. Through the foundation, they share information, provide supplies for the Charlie Diet, and support parents around the world who have children with epilepsy.

Elaine Hall was a professional acting coach when she adopted a little boy from Russia who was diagnosed with severe autism. It was then that she found her unexpected calling. She received a grant to create the Miracle Project, a musical theater program for children of all abilities. Her son's story inspired her to write a memoir, *Now I See the Moon*, which was the official selection for World Autism Awareness Day 2011 at the United Nations. HBO produced a film, *Autism, the Musical*, based on the Miracle Project, in which her son had a starring role.

In a 2014 interview, Hall reflected on her son's life and her old idea of normal.[8] "It didn't matter if he was going to be able to live a typical life, but that we would have a relationship. It was more about curing me than curing autism . . . I needed to learn how to regulate myself and find peace within my own soul . . . I want to tell parents that one day everything they have learned, they will be able to give back."

Rabbi Naomi Levy wrote about her atypical parenting journey in a touching book titled *Hope Will Find You*. In it she describes her personal journey to rediscover her true calling as a rabbi while also raising a child with a life-threatening developmental illness. At the depth of her depression and worry about her daughter, Noa, she wrote in her journal, "God believes in Noa. God believes in all people. And God is praying we will come to see in ourselves what God already sees. The God who sees me is calling, 'Where are you coming from and where are you going?'" Naomi made the choice to heed her calling and open a small synagogue. Today she has a thriving congregation and is recognized as one of the most influential rabbis in the country.

Dona Wright, the mother of an adult son with autism, did not receive the correct diagnosis for her child until he was seventeen. Her battles to get him appropriate services galvanized her, and she used the skills and knowledge she acquired to become an advocate for other parents. She volunteered to go with them to IEP meetings; she researched the law and read the assessment reports. "I had a medical background, so understanding the reports came more easily to me than it did to most parents." What began with advising her friends culminated in Wright joining a nationally recognized law firm to become a full-time advocate.

You don't need to go to law school or find a cure for autism to add meaning to your life. But you will be changed by raising your child, and you will grow. With your knowledge and skills, you can have a positive impact in your world, on whatever level feels right to you. Are you athletic? Volunteer for the Special Olympics. Do you have a background in education? Become an advocate for parents of younger children with special needs, and help them navigate the school system's services. Taking on a challenge outside your child's routine will invigorate you and move you into a life of self-confidence and action. When you're ready, when you have accepted your son or daughter and your unexpected life, I hope you will reach out and help other parents rise to their challenges, just as you have.

When You Are Ready, You Will Rise

When you're raising a child, you don't think about what he or she will be like at the age of twenty-five. But as a neuropsychologist, that is exactly what I think about when I work with a child. I tell parents, "My goal is to figure out how to help you raise a happy and successful twenty-five-year-old." They like the idea, but most can't imagine such a day. So I'd like to share one final story, told by a mother whose son was only ten:

Today was a day that I was dreading, yet another IEP meeting. Another time the teachers and principal would look at me and tell me everything that was wrong with my child. I was armed and prepared, but inside, I was shaking from nervousness. *Help me, God*, I said. *I can't go through another meeting.*

But what a surprise I got! They told me that my son, Willy, had been exited out of all of his services, as he didn't need them anymore. Things that made me cry: They said that Willy was observed on the playground for 15 minutes during recess. He was engaged in conversation with peers and also a playground group game of ball. He followed the rules of the game, engaged in conversation, made eye contact, and reacted appropriately when his turn was over.

He scored intellectually in some subjects at freshman college level. He's ten. When he was diagnosed at age four, I read everything on the Internet and felt hopeless about him ever functioning in normal society. Love, faith, perseverance, belief, and stubbornness can change everything.

Nothing is finalized, and the thought of middle school terrifies me, but just for today, I celebrate in proving wrong those people who said he would never interact, socialize, or be able to survive in a mainstream class. We are so proud of Willy for being the great kid he has grown into!

If I could look into a crystal ball and tell you, "It's all going to be okay," how would you live your life? How would that make things different for you? I want you to think about that, because the truth is, yes, you're going to work very hard and, yes, there will be good days and some very bad days, some humiliating days, some depressing days. But there will also be joyous days. And somehow you're going to get through this, and your child is going to grow, and you're going to grow with your child. Somehow, it is going to be okay. You're going to find the strength. And you can start right now. Forget that you don't feel ready. Forget that you haven't been perfect. I hope that I have given you ways to find strength in this book, but you will also find it in your friends and family, in your child's friends and teachers, and in your community.

The most important place you will find the strength to go forward is in your relationship with your child. That child has already been your teacher, your guide, and your inspiration. And you will be the person who shows your child how to love, cope, cry, struggle, celebrate, and how to live a beautiful but imperfect life. Have the courage to keep moving forward—you are worthy and you are ready. Your child already loves you for who you are. Now go make yourself and your child proud!

ACKNOWLEDGMENTS

It takes an army to raise an atypical child, and it took an army to help raise this book. I would like to express my gratitude to the many people who saw me through this book providing support, talking things over, reading, writing, offering comments, allowing me to quote their remarks, and assisting in the editing, proofreading, and design.

Thank you to my editor at Perigee/Penguin, Marian Lizzi, for signing on to this project and for her insightful guidance; to Stephanie Tade, my book agent, for her immediate understanding of the importance of this work and unflagging enthusiastic support; and the remarkable design team at Perigee/Penguin. Thank you to Alison Graham, who never misses a beat and provided so much support for this project.

I feel so incredibly lucky to be surrounded by a group of colleagues and friends who are experts in their fields and provided wisdom and guidance along this journey. Special thanks to Daniel Siegel who over the years, has patiently listened to my "left hemisphere" theories and provided personal time, suggested resources, and guidance. To Elaine Hantman and Bonnie Goldstein, two of the brightest and skilled psychotherapists I know, on opposite coasts, for their reading every word and supporting the work. For providing both research and practical application in all things mindful, thanks to Elisha Goldstein for teaching me the STOP method, and to Sylvia Boorstein for her input into the "sweetheart group" and personal modeling of compassion. I am grateful to Jaak Panksepp, for his generosity of time and insight helping me work past my initial book concept to this one, and for his brilliant insights into the world of the mammalian and human kingdoms. Thanks to Tova Yellin, for her well-earned compassionate wisdom and insights into the world of pediatric medicine and children. Thanks to Rabbi Laura Geller for sharing her spiritual insights into family dynamics and to Rabbi Jill Zimmerman and Eli Zimmerman for their insight into the world of disabilities and sharing of wisdom on the world of compassionate meditation. And to my office mate and partner in all things children, Bette Geller Jackson. Special thanks to Shifra Bemis and Bonnie Landin for their support and wisdom. Much thanks to Lynette Padwa, Beth Lieberman, and Laura Berlotti for their skills and insights. And to the folks at the Lavender Inn in Ojai, my "secret" writing place.

There are also my most amazing cheerleaders, my family and friends, and above all, my husband and best friend, Izzy, who gave me the courage to put my thoughts into print and who is my role model in courage and compassion. My wonderful kids, Dave, Josh, Deanie, and Erin, you have "inspired and rewired" me and continue to teach me more about life than I ever could imagine. And to Carly June who is a constant source of joy and amazement. To Nira Kfir and Efrat Kfir-Yehene, cousins and compatriots in the "family business" and singular experts in psychotherapy, who listened, supported, and gave insightful feedback.

To all of my clients, past and present, and other parents that I have interviewed, who have offered me time and insights, who have allowed me to quote their stories and share in the details of their lives—even if you do not recognize yourselves, thank you for your cumulative wisdom over the years. I hope you have learned as much from me as I have learned from you, and I remain eternally grateful.

BIBLIOGRAPHY

Ainsworth, Mary D. Salter, Mary C. Blehar, Everett Waters, and Sally Wall. *Patterns of Attachment: A Psychological Study of the Strange Situation.* Hillsdale, NJ: Lawrence Erlbaum, 1978.

American Psychological Association. "Supporting Psychologists' Youngest Clients." *American Psychological Association Monitor on Psychology,* July/August 2013, 44(7). apa.org/monitor/2013/07-08/youngest-clients.aspx.

Azarva, Joan M. "Learning Disabilities and Sibling Relationships." *LD OnLine,* 2010. ldonline.org/article/5847/.

Barclay, Rachel. "Why Autistic Kids Get Lost in the Details." *Healthline News,* August 9, 2013. healthline.com/health-news/mental-oxytocin-levels-may-explain-autistic-issues-080913.

Begely, Sharon. *Train Your Brain, Change Your Mind: How a New Science Reveals Our Extraordinary Potential to Transform Ourselves.* New York: Ballantine, 2007.

Blakeslee, Sandra, and Matthew Blakeslee. *The Body Has a Mind of Its Own: How Body Maps in Your Brain Help You Do (Almost) Everything Better.* New York: Random House, 2007.

Boorstein, Sylvia. *Happiness Is an Inside Job: Practicing for a Joyful Life.* New York: Ballantine, 2007.

Bowlby, John. *A Secure Base: Clinical Applications of Attachment Theory.* London: Routledge, 1988.

Brizendine, Louann. *The Female Brain.* New York: Morgan Road, 2006.

Brizendine, Louann. *The Male Brain.* New York: Crown, 2010.

Brody, Denise. *The Elephant in the Playroom: Ordinary Parents Write Intimately and Honestly About Raising Kids with Special Needs.* New York: Hudson Street, 2007.

Brown, Brené. *The Gifts of Imperfection: Let Go of Who You Think You're Supposed to Be and Embrace Who You Are*. Center City, MN: Hazelden, 2010.

Butlerbeat Mda. Elaine Hall interviewed by Scott Bridge. *Butler Beat*, April 2, 2014. youtube.com/watch?v=pxVsfeZYf8k.

Cadell, Susan, C. Regehr, and D. Hemsworth. "Factors Contributing to Post-traumatic Growth: A Proposed Structural Equation Model." *American Journal of Orthopsychiatry*, July 2003, 73(3): 279–287.

Carter, Liane Kupferberg. "Autism Acceptance: The Crucial String." *Huffington Post*, April 2, 2014. huffingtonpost.com/liane-kupferberg-carter/autism-acceptance-the-crucial-string_b_5075909.html.

Centers for Disease Control and Prevention. "Morbidity and Mortality Weekly Report (MMWR): QuickStats: Percentage of Children Aged 5–17 Years Ever Receiving a Diagnosis of Learning Disability, by Race/Ethnicity and Family Income Group—National Health Interview Survey, United States, 2007–2009." *Centers for Disease Control and Prevention Weekly*, July 1, 2011, 60(25): 853. cdc.gov/mmwr/preview/mmwrhtml/mm6025a6.htm.

The Charlie Foundation for Ketogenic Therapies. "What Is the Ketogenic Diet?" charliefoundation.org/explore-ketogenic-diet/explore-1/introducing-the-diet.

Childre, Doc, and Deborah Rozman. *Transforming Anger: The Heartmath Solution for Letting Go of Rage, Frustration, and Irritation*. Oakland, CA: New Harbinger, 2003.

Cozolino, Louis. *The Neuroscience of Human Relationships: Attachment and the Developing Social Brain*. New York: W. W. Norton, 2006.

Cozolino, Louis. *The Neuroscience of Psychotherapy: Healing the Social Brain*. New York: W. W. Norton, 2010.

Creswell, J. David, B. M. Way, N. I. Eisenberger, and M. D. Lieberman. "Neural Correlates of Dispositional Mindfulness During Affect Labeling." *Psychosomatic Medicine*, July–August 2007, 69(6): 560–565.

The Daily Beast. "The Coming Special Needs Crisis." *Newsweek*, April 29, 2012.

Damasio, Antonio. *Descartes' Error: Emotion, Reason, and the Human Brain*. New York: G. P. Putnam's Sons, 1994.

Darwin, Charles. *The Expression of the Emotions in Man and Animals*. London: John Murray, 1872.

Davidson, Richard, and Daniel Goleman. *Training the Brain: Cultivating Emotional Skills*. Northampton, MA: More Than Sound, 2012.

Davis, Andrew S., ed. *Handbook of Pediatric Neuropsychology*. New York: Springer, 2010.

Dawson, Jodie. "Learning Disabilities and Sibling Issues." GreatSchools, 2008. greatschools.org/special-education/support/680-learning-disabilities -sibling-issues.gs.

Devitt, Terry. "For Mothers of Children with Autism, the Caregiving Life Proves Stressful." *University of Wisconsin–Madison News*, November 10, 2009. news .wisc.edu/17346.

Doidge, Norman. *The Brain That Changes Itself: Stories of Personal Triumph from the Frontiers of Brain Science*. New York: Viking, 2007.

Dreifus, Claudia. "Seeking Autism's Biochemical Roots." *New York Times*, March 25, 2014: D2.

Durand, V. Mark. *Optimistic Parenting: Hope and Help for You and Your Challenging Child*. Baltimore, MD: Brookes, 2011.

Dykens, Elisabeth M., Marisa H. Fisher, Julie Lounds Taylor, Warren Lambert, and Nancy Miodrag. "Reducing Distress in Mothers of Children with Autism and Other Disabilities: A Randomized Trial." *Pediatrics*, July 21, 2014. doi: 10.1542/peds.2013-3164d.

Emerson, David, and Elizabeth Hopper. *Overcoming Trauma Through Yoga: Reclaiming Your Body*. Berkeley, CA: North Atlantic, 2011.

Fein, Deborah, Marianne Barton, Inge-Marie Eigsti, et al. "Optimal Outcome in Individuals with a History of Autism." *Journal of Child Psychology and Psychiatry*, February 2013, 54(2): 195–205. doi: 10.1111/jcpp.12037.

Frances, Allen. *Saving Normal: An Insider's Revolt Against Out-of-Control Psychiatric Diagnosis, DSM-5, Big Pharma, and the Medicalization of Ordinary Life*. New York: William Morrow, 2013.

Frankl, Viktor E. *Man's Search for Meaning*. Boston: Beacon, 2006.

Gilbert, Paul. *The Compassionate Mind: A New Approach to Life's Challenges*. Oakland, CA: New Harbinger, 2009.

Goleman, Daniel. *Emotional Intelligence: Why It Can Matter More Than IQ*. New York: Bantam, 1996.

Goleman, Daniel. *The Meditative Mind: The Varieties of Meditative Experience*. New York: Tarcher, 1988.

Graham, Linda. *Bouncing Back: Rewiring Your Brain for Maximum Resilience and Well-Being*. Novato, CA: New World Library, 2013.

Grandin, Temple. *The Autistic Brain: Thinking Across the Spectrum*. Boston: Houghton Mifflin Harcourt, 2013.

Grossman, Judy. "Family Matters: The Impact of Learning Disabilities." *LD On-Line*, 2010. ldonline.org/article/6057.

Hall, Elaine. "After Raising a Son with Severe Autism, I Have Redefined

'Normal.'" *Kveller: A Jewish Twist on Parenting*, Feb. 27, 2014. kveller.com/blog/parenting/after-raising-a-son-with-severe-autism-i-have-redefined-normal.

Hampton, Kelle. *Bloom: Finding Beauty in the Unexpected*. New York: William Morrow, 2012.

Hanson, Rick. *Hardwiring Happiness: The New Brain Science of Contentment, Calm, and Confidence*. New York: Harmony, 2013.

Harvard Mahony Neuroscience Institute. "Anger and the Brain." *On the Brain: The Harvard Mahony Neuroscience Institute Letter*, Winter 2009, 15(1).

Hayes, Steven C., and Spencer Smith. *Get Out of Your Mind and Into Your Life: The New Acceptance and Commitment Therapy*. Oakland, CA: New Harbinger, 2005.

Hayes, Steven C., Kirk D. Strosahl, and Kelly G. Wilson. *Acceptance and Commitment Therapy: The Process and Practice of Mindful Change*. New York: Guilford, 2011.

Heiman, Tali. "Parents of Children with Disabilities: Resilience, Coping and Future Expectations." *Journal of Developmental and Physical Disabilities*, June 2002, 14(2): 159–171.

Helt, Molly, Elizabeth Kelley, Marcel Kinsbourne, et al. "Can Children with Autism Recover? If So, How?" *Neuropsychology Review*, December 2008, 18(4): 339–366. doi: 10.1007/s11065-008-9075-9.

Holden, George W., and Paul Alan Williamson. "Religion and Child Well-Being." From *Handbook of Child Well-Being: Theories, Methods and Policies in Global Perspective*, Asher Ben-Arieh, Ferran Casas, Ivar Frones, Jill E. Korbin, eds. New York: Springer, 2014: 1137–1169.

Hughes, Daniel A., and Jonathan Baylin. *Brain-Based Parenting: The Neuroscience of Caregiving for Healthy Attachment*. New York: W. W. Norton, 2012.

Iacoboni, Marco. *Mirroring People: The New Science of How We Connect with Others*. New York: Farrar, Straus and Giroux, 2008.

Jarrett, Christian. "How Becoming a Father Changes Your Brain." *Wired*, July 17, 2014.

Johnson, Lynn D. *Enjoy Life!: Healing with Happiness*. Head Acre, 2007.

Johnson, Lynn D. *Get on the Peace Train: A Journey from Anger to Harmony*. Head Acre, 2007.

Jones, Lisa, Mark A. Bellis, Sara Wood, et al. "Prevalence and Risk of Violence Against Children with Disabilities: A Systematic Review and Meta-Analysis of Observational Studies." *Lancet*, September 8, 2012, 380(9845): 899–907. doi: 10.1016/S0140-6736(12)60692-8.

Joseph, Stephen, and Lisa D. Butler. "Positive Changes Following Adversity." *PTSD Research Quarterly*, 21(3), Summer 2010.

Kearney, Penelope M., and Tim Griffin. "Between Joy and Sorrow: Being a Parent of a Child with Developmental Disability." *Journal of Advanced Nursing*, 2001, 34(5): 582–592. doi: 10.1046/j.1365-2648.2001.01787.x.

Kennedy, Kimberly. "Personal Growth in Couples Caring for a Child with a Life-Threatening Illness." *Theses and Dissertations (Comprehensive)*. Paper 938, 2009.

Klass, Perri. "Haunted by a Child's Illness." *New York Times*, Oct. 15, 2013: D6.

Klass, Perri. "Parents' Depression Linked to Problems in Children." *New York Times*, May 7, 2012. well.blogs.nytimes.com/2012/05/07/parents-depression-linked-to-problems-in-children/?_r=0.

Kornfield, Jack. *The Wise Heart: A Guide to the Universal Teachings of Buddhist Psychology*. New York: Bantam, 2008.

Larson, Elizabeth. "Reframing the Meaning of Disability to Families: The Embrace of Paradox." *Social Science & Medicine*, October 1, 1998, 47(7): 865–875.

Leder, Drew, and Mitchell W. Krucoff. "'Take Your Pill': The Role and Fantasy of Pills in Modern Medicine." *The Journal of Alternative and Complementary Medicine*, June 2014, 20(6): 421–427. doi:10.1089/acm.2013.0447.

Ledoux, Joseph. *The Emotional Brain: The Mysterious Underpinnings of Emotional Life*. New York: Simon & Schuster, 1998.

Levy, Naomi. *Hope Will Find You: My Search for the Wisdom to Stop Waiting and Start Living*. New York: Harmony, 2010.

Lieber, Ron. "The Psychic Toll Paid in a Special Needs House." *New York Times*, October 13, 2012: B1.

MacVean, Mary. "A Grateful State: Gratitude Is Vital to Well-Being, Research Shows." *Los Angeles Times*, November 17, 2012.

McNeil Jr., Donald G. "Assault: Children with Disabilities Are More Likely to Be Victims of Violence, Analysis Shows." *New York Times*, July 17, 2012: D6.

Miller, Nancy B. *Nobody's Perfect: Living and Growing with Children Who Have Special Needs*. Baltimore: P. H. Brookes, 1994.

Miodrag, Nancy, and Robert M. Hodapp. "Chronic Stress and Health Among Parents of Children with Intellectual and Developmental Disabilities." *Current Opinion in Psychiatry*, September 2010, 23(5): 407–411. doi: 10.1097/YCO.0b013e32833a8796.

Nagasawa, Miho, Kazutaka Mogi, and Takefumi Kikusui. "Attachment Between Humans and Dogs." *Japanese Psychological Research*, Special Issue: Divergence of Comparative Cognitive Studies in Japan, September 2009, 51(3): 209–221. onlinelibrary.wiley.com/doi/10.1111/j.1468-5884.2009.00402.x/full.

National Survey of Children's Health, 2011/2012. Data Resource Center for Child and Adolescent Health. childhealthdata.org/browse/survey? q=2456&r=1.

Natterson-Horowitz, Barbara, and Kathryn Bowers. *Zoobiquity: What Animals Can Teach Us About Health and the Science of Healing.* New York: Alfred A. Knopf, 2012.

Neal, Elizabeth G., Hannah Chaffe, Ruby H. Schwartz, et al. "The Ketogenic Diet for the Treatment of Childhood Epilepsy: A Randomised Controlled Trial." *Lancet Neurology,* June 2008; 7(6): 500–506. doi: 10.1016/S1474 -4422(08)70092-9.

Neff, Kristin. *Self-Compassion: Stop Beating Yourself Up and Leave Insecurity Behind.* New York: HarperCollins, 2011.

Ogden, Pat, Kekuni Minton, Clare Pain, and Daniel J. Siegel. *Trauma and the Body: A Sensorimotor Approach to Psychotherapy.* New York: W. W. Norton, 2006.

Olmert, Meg Daly. *Made for Each Other: The Biology of the Human-Animal Bond.* Cambridge, MA: Da Capo, 2009.

Ornstein, Robert, with David Sobel. *The Healing Brain: Breakthrough Discoveries About How the Brain Keeps Us Healthy.* New York: Simon & Schuster, 1987.

Osborne, Lisa A., Louise McHugh, Jo Saunders, and Phil Reed. "Parenting Stress Reduces the Effectiveness of Early Teaching Interventions for Autistic Spectrum Disorders." *Journal of Autism and Developmental Disorders,* July 2008, 38 (6): 1092–1103.

Osman, Betty B. "My Brother Is Different." *LD OnLine,* 2010. ldonline.org/ article/6059/.

Panksepp, Jaak. *Affective Neuroscience: The Foundations of Human and Animal Emotions.* New York: Oxford University Press, 1998.

Panksepp, Jaak, and Lucy Biven. *The Archaeology of Mind: Neuroevolutionary Origins of Human Emotions.* New York: W. W. Norton, 2012.

Pinker, Steven. *How the Mind Works.* New York: W. W. Norton, 1999.

Potter-Efron, Ronald. *Healing the Angry Brain: How Understanding the Way Your Brain Works Can Help You Control Anger and Aggression.* Oakland, CA: New Harbinger, 2012.

Poulin, Michael J., E. Alison Holman, and Anneke Buffone. "The Neurogenetics of Nice: Receptor Genes for Oxytocin and Vasopressin Interact with

Threat to Predict Prosocial Behavior." Published online before print March 28, 2012. *Psychological Science*, May 2012, 23(5): 446–452. doi: 10.1177/095679761142847.

Ratey, John. *Spark: The Revolutionary New Science of Exercise and the Brain*. New York: Little, Brown, 2008.

Rattue, Grace. "One in Four Disabled Children Likely to Be Victims of Violence." *Medical News Today*, July 14, 2012. medicalnewstoday.com/articles/247835 .php.

"Resilience: What Is Resilience?" *This Emotional Life*. PBS.org. pbs.org/this emotionallife/topic/resilience/what-resilience.

Schultz, Philip. *My Dyslexia*. New York: W. W. Norton, 2011.

Seligman, Martin E. P. "What Is Well Being?" *Authentic Happiness*, April 2011. www.authentichappiness.sas.upenn.edu/learn/wellbeing.

Seligman, Martin E. P. *Flourish: A Visionary New Understanding of Happiness and Well-Being*. New York: Free Press, 2011.

Seligman, Martin E. P. *The Optimistic Child: A Proven Program to Safeguard Children Against Depression and Build Lifelong Resilience*. New York: Houghton Mifflin, 1996.

Seltzer, Leon. "What Your Anger May Be Hiding." *Psychology Today*, July 11, 2008. psychologytoday.com/blog/evolution-the-self/200807/what-your -anger-may-be-hiding.

Shermer, Michael. "Opting Out of Overoptimism." *Scientific American*, March 2012.

Siegel, Daniel J. *Mindsight: The New Science of Personal Transformation*. New York: Bantam, 2010.

Siegel, Daniel J. *Pocket Guide to Interpersonal Neurobiology: An Integrative Handbook of the Mind*. New York: W. W. Norton, 2012.

Siegel, Daniel J., and Mary Hartzell. *Parenting from the Inside Out: How a Deeper Self-Understanding Can Help You Raise Children Who Thrive*. New York: Tarcher, 2003.

Solomon, Andrew. *Far from the Tree: Parents, Children, and the Search for Identity*. New York: Scribner, 2012.

Southwick, Steven M., and Dennis S. Charney. "Ready for Anything." *Scientific American Mind*, July/August 2013: 32.

Stahl, Bob, and Elisha Goldstein. *A Mindfulness-Based Stress Reduction Workbook*. Oakland, CA: New Harbinger, 2010.

Taylor, Shelley. *The Tending Instinct: Women, Men and the Biology of Our Relationships*. New York: Henry Holt, 2002.

Tedeschi, Richard G., and Lawrence Calhoun. "Posttraumatic Growth: A New Perspective on Psychotraumatology." *Psychiatric Times*, April 1, 2004.

University of Virginia School of Medicine. "Wisdom Through Adversity: About Our Work." medicine.virginia.edu/community-service/centers/wisdom/our-work.

Van der Kolk, Bessel A., Alexander C. McFarlane, and Lars Weisaeth, eds. *Traumatic Stress: The Effects of Overwhelming Experience on Mind, Body, and Society.* New York: Guilford, 1996.

Van Ijzendoorn, M. H., A. H. Rutgers, M. J. Bakermans-Kranenburg, et al. "Parental Sensitivity and Attachment in Children with Autism Spectrum Disorder: Comparison with Children with Mental Retardation, with Language Delays, and with Typical Development." *Child Development*, 78: 597–608. doi: 10.1111/j.1467-8624.2007.01016.x

Waisman Center, *News and Noteworthy*, November 10, 2009. waisman.wisc.edu/news/SELTZER6.HTML.

Weintraub, Amy. *Yoga for Depression: A Compassionate Guide to Relieve Suffering Through Yoga.* New York: Harmony, 2003.

Weissman, Myrna M., and Peter Jensen. "What Research Suggests for Depressed Women with Children." *Journal of Clinical Psychiatry*, July 2002, 63 (7): 641–647.

Winter, Judy. *Breakthrough Parenting for Children with Special Needs: Raising the Bar of Expectations.* San Francisco: Jossey-Bass, 2006.

Wise, Jeff. *Extreme Fear: The Science of Your Mind in Danger.* New York: Palgrave Macmillan, 2009.

Wong, Ying, and Jeanne Tsai. "Cultural Models of Shame and Guilt." In *Handbook of Self-Conscious Emotions*, J. Tracy, R. Robins, and J. Tangney, eds. New York: Guilford, 2007: 210–223. www-psych.stanford.edu/~tsailab/PDF/yw07sce.pdf.

Yates, Susan. *And Then I Had Kids: Encouragement for Mothers of Young Children.* Grand Rapids, MI: Baker, 2002.

NOTES

INTRODUCTION

1. Perri Klass, "Parents' Depression Linked to Problems in Children," *New York Times*, May 7, 2012, well.blogs.nytimes.com/2012/05/07/parents-depression-linked-to-problems-in-children/?_r=0.
2. Ibid.
3. Ibid.

1. WHAT WE EXPECT WHEN WE'RE EXPECTING

1. Daniel J. Siegel and Mary Hartzell, *Parenting from the Inside Out: How a Deeper Self-Understanding Can Help You Raise Children Who Thrive* (New York: Tarcher, 2003), 102.
2. Daniel J. Siegel, *Mindsight: The New Science of Personal Transformation* (New York: Bantam, 2011).
3. J. David Creswell et al., "Neural Correlates of Dispositional Mindfulness During Affect Labeling," *Psychosomatic Medicine*, July–August 2007, 69(6): 560–565.
4. Ying Wong and Jeanne Tsai, "Cultural Models of Shame and Guilt," from *Handbook of Self-Conscious Emotions*, J. Tracy, R. Robins, and J. Tangney, eds. (New York: Guilford, 2007), 210–223, psych.stanford.edu/~tsailab/PDF/yw07sce.pdf.
5. Deborah Fein et al., "Optimal Outcome in Individuals with a History of Autism," *Journal of Child Psychology and Psychiatry*, February 2013, 54(2): 195–205, doi: 10.1111/jcpp.12037. Molly Helt et al., "Can Children with Autism Recover? If So, How?" *Neuropsychology Review*, December 2008, 18(4): 339–366, doi: 10.1007/s11065-008-9075-9.

2. THE DENIAL PHASE

1. Pat Ogden et al., *Trauma and the Body: A Sensorimotor Approach to Psychotherapy* (New York: W. W. Norton, 2006), 14.

2. Ibid, 93.

3. Jaak Panksepp, *Affective Neuroscience: The Foundations of Human and Animal Emotions* (New York: Oxford University Press, 1998), 208.

4. Louis Cozolino, *The Neuroscience of Human Relationships: Attachment and the Developing Social Brain* (New York: W. W. Norton, 2006), 29.

3. ANGER AND BLAME

1. Paul Gilbert, *The Compassionate Mind: A New Approach to Life's Challenges* (Oakland, CA: New Harbinger, 2009), 129.

2. Jaak Panksepp and Lucy Biven, *The Archaeology of Mind: Neuroevolutionary Origins of Human Emotions* (New York: W. W. Norton, 2012).

3. Daniel Goleman, *Emotional Intelligence: Why It Can Matter More Than IQ* (New York: Bantam, 1996).

4. Ibid.

5. Centers for Disease Control and Prevention, "Morbidity and Mortality Weekly Report (MMWR): QuickStats: Percentage of Children Aged 5–17 Years Ever Receiving a Diagnosis of Learning Disability, by Race/Ethnicity and Family Income Group—National Health Interview Survey, United States, 2007–2009," *Centers for Disease Control and Prevention Weekly*, July 1, 2011, 60(25): 853, cdc.gov/mmwr/preview/mmwrhtml/mm6025a6.htm.

6. Lisa Jones et al., "Prevalence and Risk of Violence Against Children with Disabilities: A Systematic Review and Meta-Analysis of Observational Studies," *Lancet*, September 8, 2012, 380(9845): 899–907, doi: 10.1016/S0140-6736(12)60692-8.

7. Louann Brizendine, *The Female Brain* (New York: Morgan Road, 2006), 54–55.

8. Ibid.

9. Michael J. Poulin, E. Alison Holman, and Anneke Buffone, "The Neurogenetics of Nice: Receptor Genes for Oxytocin and Vasopressin Interact with Threat to Predict Prosocial Behavior," published online before print March 28, 2012, *Psychological Science*, May 2012, 23(5): 446–452, doi: 10.1177/095679761142847.

10. Rachel Barclay, "Why Autistic Kids Get Lost in the Details," *Healthline News*, August 9, 2013, healthline.com/health-news/mental-oxytocin-levels-may-explain-autistic-issues-080913.

11. Brizendine, *The Female Brain*, 102.

12. Meg Daly Olmert, *Made for Each Other: The Biology of the Human-Animal Bond* (Cambridge, MA: Da Capo, 2009), 73: "When rats are massaged for 5 minutes, the raise in oxytocin is similar to an oxytocin injection. Massage has an anti-stress response even in rats!"

13. Ibid.

14. Louann Brizendine, *The Male Brain* (New York: Crown, 2010).

15. Daniel J. Siegel, *Pocket Guide to Interpersonal Neurobiology: An Integrative Handbook of the Mind* (New York: W. W. Norton, 2012), 24–25.

16. Miho Nagasawa, Kazutaka Mogi, and Takefumi Kikusui, "Attachment Between Humans and Dogs," *Japanese Psychological Research*, Special Issue: Divergence of comparative cognitive studies in Japan, September 2009, 51(3): 209–221, onlinelibrary.wiley.com/doi/10.1111/j.1468-5884.2009.00402.x/full.

4. BARGAINING AND SEEKING SOLUTIONS

1. Panksepp and Biven, *The Archaeology of Mind*, 95–144.

2. Ibid, 106.

3. Robert Ornstein and David Sobel, *The Healing Brain: Breakthrough Discoveries About How the Brain Keeps Us Healthy* (New York: Simon & Schuster, 1987), 115.

4. Ibid, 115.

5. Panksepp and Biven, *The Archaeology of Mind*, 109.

6. Elizabeth G. Neal et al., "The Ketogenic Diet for the Treatment of Childhood Epilepsy: A Randomised Controlled Trial," *The Lancet Neurology*, June 2008, 7(6): 500–506, doi: 10.1016/S1474-4422(08)70092-9.

7. The Charlie Foundation for Ketogenic Therapies. "What Is the Ketogenic Diet?" charliefoundation.org/explore-ketogenic-diet/explore-1/introducing-the-diet.

5. THE DEPRESSION TRAP

1. Bessel A. van der Kolk, Alexander C. McFarlane, and Lars Weisaeth, eds. *Traumatic Stress: The Effects of Overwhelming Experience on Mind, Body, and Society*, (New York: Guilford, 1996), 4.

2. Allen Frances, *Saving Normal: An Insider's Revolt Against Out-of-Control Psychiatric Diagnosis, DSM-5, Big Pharma, and the Medicalization of Ordinary Life* (New York: William Morrow, 2013), 30.

3. M. H. Van Ijzendoorn, A. H. Rutgers, M. J. Bakermans-Kranenburg, et al. "Parental Sensitivity and Attachment in Children with Autism Spectrum Disorder: Comparison with Children with Mental Retardation, with Language Delays, and with Typical Development," *Child Development*, 2007, 78: 597–608, doi: 10.1111/j.1467-8624.2007.01016.x.

4. Dykens et al, "Reducing Distress in Mothers of Children with Autism and Other Disabilities: A Randomized Trial," *Pediatrics* 2014, 134(2): e454–e463.

5. Daniel J. Siegel, anecdotal, YouTube, May 18, 2011.

6. Panksepp, *The Archaeology of Mind*, 324.

7. Kristin Neff, TEDx Talk, "The Space Between Self-Esteem and Self-Compassion."

8. Myrna M. Weissman and Peter Jensen, "What Research Suggests for Depressed Women with Children," *Journal of Clinical Psychiatry*, July 2002, 641–647.

9. Ibid.

6. ACTIVE ACCEPTANCE

1. Liane Kupferberg Carter, "Autism Acceptance: The Crucial String," *Huffington Post*, April 2, 2014, huffingtonpost.com/liane-kupferberg-carter/autism-acceptance-the-crucial-string_b_5075909.html.

2. Elizabeth Larson, "Reframing the Meaning of Disability to Families: The Embrace of Paradox," *Social Science & Medicine*, October 1, 1998, 47(7): 865–875.

3. Ibid.

4. Penelope M. Kearney and Tim Griffin, "Between Joy and Sorrow: Being a Parent of a Child with Developmental Disability," *Journal of Advanced Nursing*, 2001, 34(5): 582–592, doi: 10.1046/j.1365-2648.2001.01787.x.

5. "Resilience: What Is Resilience?" *This Emotional Life*, PBS.org. pbs.org/this emotionallife/topic/resilience/what-resilience.

6. Richard G. Tedeschi and Lawrence Calhoun, "Posttraumatic Growth: A New Perspective on Psychotraumatology," *Psychiatric Times*, April 1, 2004. psychiatrictimes.com/ptsd/posttraumatic-growth-new-perspective-psychotrau matology-0#sthash.6Iz6z8hg.dpuf.

7. George W. Holden and Paul Alan Williamson, "Religion and Child Well-Being," from *Handbook of Child Well-Being: Theories, Methods and Policies in Global Perspective*, Asher Ben-Arieh et al., eds. (New York: Springer, 2014), 1137–1169.

8. Butlerbeat Mda, Elaine Hall interviewed by Scott Bridge, *Butler Beat*, April 2, 2014, youtube.com/watch?v=pxVsfeZYf8k.

INDEX

Page numbers in *italics* indicate tables.

ABOUT THE AUTHOR

Dr. Rita Eichenstein is a noted psychologist, neuropsychologist, and author who has been in clinical practice for over twenty years. In addition to running a thriving private practice in both pediatric neuropsychology and psychotherapy for children, teens, young adults, parents, and families at Cedars-Sinai Medical Center in Los Angeles, Dr. Eichenstein has lectured at schools, organizations, and media across the United States. Dr. Eichenstein has been married for more than twenty-five years, having raised three children and numerous dogs. She blogs on mental health issues at PositivelyAtypical.com.